The residential community

Library of Social Work

General Editor:
Noel Timms
Professor of Social Work Studies
University of Newcastle upon Tyne

The residential community

A setting for social work

Howard Jones

Professor of Social Administration
University College, Cardiff

HV
9145
. A5
J66x
WEST

Routledge & Kegan Paul
London, Boston and Henley

ASU WEST LIBRARY

First published in 1979
by Routledge & Kegan Paul Ltd
39 Store Street,
London WC1E 7DD,
Broadway House,
Newtown Road,
Henley-on-Thames,
Oxon RG9 1EN and
9 Park Street,
Boston, Mass. 02108, USA
Set in 10/11 pt English
and printed in Great Britain by
The Lavenham Press Limited
Lavenham, Suffolk
© Howard Jones 1979

British Library Cataloguing in Publication Data

Jones, Howard, b. 1918
The residential community.—(Library of
social work).
1. Juvenile detention homes—Great Britain
I. Title   II. Series
365'.42   HV9146   78-40906

ISBN 0 7100 0122 3
ISBN 0 7100 0123 1 Pbk

Contents

Chapter one

Antecedents

Residential social work is concerned with service to persons who for one reason or another cannot have their social needs met while living at home. So they reside in a substitute home run by a social work agency, and the social work service is provided as part of a twenty-four-hours-a-day ongoing regime, in which going to bed at night and getting up in the morning, meal-times, daily ablutions and recreational and educational programmes may all have a part to play, as well as personal counselling of the kind which is more readily recognisable as social work.

The extent to which these daily routines are integrated with the more specifically social work aims of the residential institution varies. Where they are fully integrated the institution in question has become what is now sometimes called a 'therapeutic community'. In most cases, however, the connection between the two though real is less systematically and fully developed. Thus in a therapeutic community, the rehabilitation, say, of the boys in a school for delinquents is not seen as confined to certain parts of the programme: education, religious observance, casework sessions, rewards and punishments. Instead it is argued that everything that happens to the boys while living at the school has its impact upon them and must therefore be planned to ensure that the impact is a beneficial one. In institutions which do not aim to be therapeutic communities, these experiences are seen as merely part of the context within which therapy must proceed. Children must have regular and nutritious meals, must get enough sleep, must be kept clean; and all these things must happen within a stable framework of order. When all this can be taken for granted, the training or therapeutic activity can proceed without hindrance. As will be seen later, there is much overlap between these two kinds of institution. Nevertheless they do represent very different viewpoints about the

1

nature of residential care, and raise important issues which must be discussed in more detail later on.

What types of residential provision fall within the scope of residential social work? There is first of all a grey area called 'boarding-out', or in the case of children, 'fostering'. This usually involves placing the client to live with a family in their home, with the idea of providing as near an approximation to family life as possible. This is not residential social work as the term is normally used. The family in question are not social workers, and indeed if they behaved as social workers would destroy some of the specific virtues of boarding-out — its spontaneity and immediacy as a human and social experience. It is as a member of a real family displaying the natural feelings and attitudes of a family that the client is expected to benefit. However, boarding-out in this pure form does begin to merge into residential social work in those cases where a family undertakes the care of a number of clients at the same time, so that for some member of the family (usually the housewife) it become virtually a full-time job. It then begins to be difficult to distinguish between boarding-out, and the small, family-group home, located in an ordinary street, and run by a full-time residential social worker. Some kind of training like that provided for residential social workers may well be the next step. Similar considerations apply to the sheltered housing provided for the elderly by some local authorities. A group of old people's bungalows is supervised by a warden who lives nearby. Usually her emoluments are limited and she is expected only to keep a rather more than usually neighbourly eye on the old folks.

If residential social work is not to include boarding-out and sheltered housing what is it concerned with? It includes, of course, children's homes[1] of all kinds, ranging from the family-group home already referred to, to larger establishments often set in their own grounds. Some will be homes for difficult[2] or delinquent[3] and others for blind, deaf, or mentally or physically handicapped children — or for children with no other handicap than that nevertheless grievous handicap of having no one to love or care for them. Some children's homes may be intended for short stays only, while others can expect to have their children until they are grown-up and independent. Each of these types of home obviously presents special problems related to the nature of their inmate populations and the purposes they have set for themselves.

And so far we have mentioned only institutions for children. Consider the variety in types of provision for old people,[4] ranging from modern purpose-built homes to barrack-type former poor-law institutions, and from large efficiently run establishments providing constant care and many services for their residents, to a converted villa in a city street, divided into bed-sitters in which old people cook their own food and run their own lives under the benevolent eye of a residential care worker who intervenes only when it seems necessary.

Residential care for children has received much more attention in the past than that for the elderly, but there are signs that we are at last recognising the nature of the demographic changes that are now upon us. We are all living longer, and the number of old people in the population is increasing rapidly. The figures in Table 1 show clearly enough the size of the present problem, and the shape of things to come. The relative increase projected in the numbers of the very old is particularly noteworthy. The days of the self-sacrificing, unmarried daughter, or the daughter-in-law who has time to look after granny because she has no job outside the home, are past. And even if they were not, the burden represented by much older, old people, subject to more disabilities, is likely to be unacceptable to a generation which is less kin-centred and more impatient for gratification than previous ones. So a larger proportion of this larger number of old people in the population are going to require the help of the social services, including residential care. In the future the care of old people is likely to represent the larger part of the residential social worker's task.

TABLE 1   *Population trends, UK*[5]

Thousands	1951	1971	1981	2001
Aged at least 75	2392	2610	3136	3535
Aged at least 85	227	478	545	744

Some reference has already been made to institutions for delinquent children, but institutions for older offenders ought probably also to be included. Some will question whether prisons or borstals are social work institutions at all, and much here depends upon one's penal or correctional philosophy. If you believe that the only proper aims for a penal system are retribution (dealing out to a criminal his 'just deserts'), or deterrence (punishing him to the point that he comes to feel that crime is not worthwhile) then there is little scope for social work. Others, like Sir Rupert Cross,[6] while seeing no objection on moral grounds to setting a rehabilitative target for the penal system, will question its practicability. They will point to the pressures for criminal contamination in prison, the long-standing tradition of hostility between staff and inmates; and the containment policies which so easily produce institutionalised old lags. Surely all that can be done in the face of so many sources of

3

contamination, is to prevent the prison from doing its inmates too much harm. Not all (including the present writer) will agree with this pessimistic point of view; but even if it were to be accepted, there would still be an important role for social work in countering the various corrupting factors at work in the prisons.

In all the types of residential institutions so far discussed, the social work task could be seen as primary. Providing social care for children or old people, and rehabilitation for offenders, is the purpose for which the institution exists. Many other people are of course involved — cooks, domestic staff, gardeners, etc. — but their work, though essential, is ancillary to the main social work task. Nevertheless, co-ordinated team work is vital. For example, the kitchen can be the core of the life of a small children's home, and if the cook's views of the way in which children should be trained differ from those of other members of staff, the effectiveness of the institution could be seriously impaired. The question of team work will be taken up again in Chapter 10.

In hospitals, on the other hand, the social work task is not the main *raison d'être* of the institution. One exception to this ought to be certain geriatric wards, where the natural degenerative processes of ageing, about which little can be done, present more limited scope for medical treatment, than exist in the acute wards. Nursing, and a watching brief for the doctor, are usually all that can be utilised. Instead the emphasis should be shifted to the maintenance of the patient's personality by means of activities and social interaction. This is really a task for the residential social worker, and it is rarely adequately attempted because of the fallacious assumption that the primary need of these individuals is medical in character.

Social work is also probably more central in the mental hospital than in hospitals for the physically ill, for mental illness may sometimes arise in part out of the social stress which it is the job of the social worker to understand and to relieve. In other words, social work may sometimes be as essential to the care of a mental patient as the psychotherapy, drugs, or surgery administered by the medical staff. In other kinds of mental disorder, where genetic or organic pathologies predominate, it will be less important, fulfilling only a secondary role, in support of the medical function of the hospital. And this is, of course, usually the case in non-mental hospitals.

Current thinking nevertheless sees social work in hospitals as much more than merely reassuring worried relatives, dealing with a patient's pension, or obtaining an appliance for him.[7] There is an important psycho-social element in most illnesses, and the doctor who recognises this, values the assistance of his social worker as much as that of his nurses. What has not been so fully acknowledged is the value of the residential social worker (as distinct from that of the social caseworker) and yet the hospital is a residential institution, the regime of which must play an important part in deciding whether the patient recovers quickly or not. An important early demonstration of the truth of this was the Northfield Experiment with psychiatric casualties during the Second World War,[8] and there have been many subsequent enterprises along similar lines, notably the work which has been carried out for so long at the Henderson Hospital in Surrey.[9] But all of these have been in the field of psychiatry; the increasing (and justified) prestige of psycho-social medicine makes it necessary now to begin to extend the concepts of residential social work, at least in a valuable ancillary role, to other kinds of hospital.

The prototypes of the residential institution were probably the county gaols, the bridewells of the sixteenth century, and the work-houses established within the Poor Law under the Statute of Elizabeth in 1601 as a means of caring for and training the poor. With the tightening up of the Poor Law in the nineteenth century and to deter people from pauperism, a stigma was attached to the workhouse; and partly for this reason and partly because of the recognition of the need for new forms of relief, children's homes, old people's homes and infirmaries, which were still part of poor-law provision, began to separate out from the workhouse proper.[10] Parallel with this development came the movement to get young offenders out of prison into special institutions.[11] Such reformatories run by private charitable organisations, though few before 1850, increased rapidly in number as they gained legal recognition in the 1950s and 1960s. Industrial schools, for younger delinquents and for deprived children, followed. Asylums for the insane have existed for centuries. Bethlem in London was being used for lunatics from the beginning of the fifteenth century. These early institutions were hardly hospitals, however, but places of confinement. Henderson and Gillespie date the modern era only from the end of the eighteenth century.[12]

By the end of the nineteenth century most of these residential establishments had begun to conform to a common pattern. They were large and organised for mass living, with rigid rules and discipline. Inmates were either (as in the case of prisons or asylums or even some workhouses) confined in cells; or in other institutions were congregated together in large dormitories and day rooms. They had imposed on them highly institutionalised styles of life, cutting them off from the normal community so that their lives and attitudes were entirely bounded by the walls of the institution itself. Even after many children's and old people's homes and many of the infirmaries had been hived-off from the Poor Law to become in effect separate welfare services this pattern persisted in them to a large extent. It represented the barracks type of institution from which we have been trying to escape ever since.

Some at first saw such an escape as a possibility, through the sub-division of large institutions into cottages or villas; and later by replacing larger institutions by scattered homes or hostels — small family-size groups looked after in ordinary houses located here and there in ordinary streets. However, from the 1950s onwards a new orthodoxy was becoming prevalent to the effect that residential establishments of all kinds were incurably institutionalising, and that we would therefore do better to try to keep people out of them. Among the earlier influences of this kind was the research in the 1950s of Bowlby and Robertson,[13] which suggested that the emotional development of young children, and therefore their social adjustment, was sometimes seriously impaired by lengthy periods of impersonal, institutional residence. Although statutory recognition of these ideas had to await the passing of the Children and Young Persons Act 1968, they had already by this time had a tremendous impact on child care policy in relation to both homes and hostels. Boarding-out, and the treatment of sick children at home (or at least the de-institutionalising of children's hospitals), had become the desirable norm.

The Mental Health Act 1959, also, among many other things, included provisions designed to encourage the care of mental patients within the community. This gave legal expression to developments in treatment aimed at using drugs to achieve 'social adjustment' rather than cure; the implication being that the period of hospitalisation could therefore be short, even if it had to be repeated from time to time as symptoms recurred.

In some ways it was ironical that the mental hospital should have been such an early target of the anti-institution movement, as British mental hospitals, at any rate, following a series of reforming acts before the war, were far-removed from the *Snake Pit* image presented by some of their American counterparts. The lack of sufficient social work support also meant, as such writers as Richard Titmuss pointed out,[14] that patients were in danger of receiving treatment inferior to that which could have been provided for them in hospital. And, it might be added, undue pressures were placed on relatives.

The technical developments in drug therapy which made it possible to move towards community care in psychiatry had its counterpart in general medicine, particularly in surgery, where short-term hospitalisation was becoming the rule.

The apathy and impersonality of old people's homes, many of them still run in the same unfeeling way and often in the same buildings as under the Poor Law, was widely recognised by the early post-war period, but the real pressure for reform began only with the publication in 1962 of Peter Townsend's *The Last Refuge*.[15] Many of the old-style institutions were renovated as a result, and the trend towards purpose-built homes, often giving the old people much more independence than had been customary in the past, received a fillip. More significant in the present context, however, was the emergence here also of the community care concept — providing old people with domestic and social help to enable them to stay in their own homes as long as possible, or at worst in sheltered housing units.

The attack on the institutional approach within the penal system was mounted from a number of different directions. We have already seen how the work of Dr Bowlby and his collaborators produced a revulsion against residential homes for children, and this affected residential correctional schools as much as it did homes for deprived children who had not committed offences. As a result there was a steep decline in the number of committals to approved schools in the late 1950s. Many schools were closed, causing some difficulty when delinquency increased steeply a few years later. However, the anti-institution ideology had lost none of its force, and when the new Children and Young Persons Act 1968 was passed it set about not only to remove children wherever possible from the operation of the penal law and the penal system, but to ensure also that wherever possible they were dealt with at home through family casework. Thus approved school committals were abolished and replaced by a care order, which enabled a Social Services Department of a local authority to have a child placed away from home if they felt this was desirable, but could refrain from doing so if they felt that treatment at home was preferable. One of the complaints made by magistrates against the way in which the 1968 Act is operating, is that Social Services Departments do not have delinquent children sent away consistently enough to provide what they see as a necessary deterrent. But such complaints are concerned with punishment rather than rehabilitation. And we have a long way to go before we replace the institution to the extent that some American states have done, for example, Massachusetts, which abolished juvenile correctional institutions by fiat, thus compelling the responsible officials to find alternative solutions.

Prisons as we have seen have long been considered to have a deleterious effect on those confined in them. The relative costliness of keeping a man locked-up for a period of years, as compared with non-custodial solutions, is also very telling. All residential care is expensive, of course, as compared with care in the community — even where the very costly security measures of the prison are not required. Ironically, the fact that in Britain, as in other countries, the penal system is a Cinderella on which governments are not willing to spend money unless they have to, operates as an influence in favour of penal reform. For whatever may be the case with other kinds of residential institutions, imprisonment does seem to be damaging, and avoiding it is therefore in itself a desirable reform, even though the reasons for carrying it out may be financial.

The Criminal Justice Act 1967 made the first serious inroads into imprisonment by developing the concept of the suspended sentence — to be imposed if the person committed further offences during the time prescribed. This may not have had quite the effect intended: people given suspended sentences who then fell by the wayside tended to get longer sentences as a result, thus actually increasing the prison population. But at least the implementation of the idea of parole,[16] though not keeping people out of prison, did have the effect of *getting* some of them out sooner than would otherwise have been the case. The Criminal Justice Act 1972 introduced two further kinds of disposition as alternatives to sentences of imprisonment: the community service order,[17] and attendance at a day training centre as a condition of probation.[18] Parole was started cautiously, but now (though its mode of operation leaves much to be desired) seems to be making more of an impact on prison populations. Day training centres have still to make their mark, but community service looks as if it may prove to be a genuine breakthrough.

The main charge against residential establishments has, throughout, been that they institutionalise their inmates, thus unfitting them for non-institutional life. The concept of institutionalisation[19] plays such a central role in thinking about residential care that it justifies a fairly detailed analysis.

There would be general agreement first of all that it arises out of an adaptation by the inmates to the regime of the institution. This makes life easier for both the staff and the inmate himself; both know where they stand, and can settle down into a tranquil routine. On the other hand, it is this very adjustment to life 'inside', which is said to disable the inmate from surviving outside. Shut off from normal society, he acquires habits and attitudes which are functional only within the institution.

Most of the blame is usually attributed to the regimentation of institutional life. Such places run 'like a clock'. There is a time for everything, and rules as to how everything is to be done. While certainly simplifying life for all concerned, it also means that residents need to assume little or no responsibility for themselves. There is always a bell or a staff member to remind them; and as the daily routine is so inexorable, habit encouraged by a system of rewards and punishments gradually takes over. Small wonder if they eventually become dependent on this massive framework of support, and terrified at the thought of going out into the world and standing once again on their own feet.

The picture conjured up by this account is of the happy resident, knowing all the rules and keeping them; and living a healthy, well-fed and well-ordered existence. He would have no desire for an independent life, it is true, and would also be subject to severe limitations of personal experience within the institution, but on the whole he would be contented, and safe from the dangers which had brought him into residential care in the first place. Some individuals of a dependent and adaptable disposition might make this kind of adjustment, but there are forces at work which can set off in other residents rather more debilitating trends.

Although these trends are all properly described by the word 'deprivation', they take a number of different forms. For instance the efficient organisation of the old-style institution led to a depersonalisation of the regime. Just as the economies of mass production in the modern car industry are obtained by means of a process of standardisation in which all the cars produced are identical, with parts fully interchangeable between them, so human beings in the barracks style institution were assumed to be identical. They did not need to be treated as individual personalities, but simply as units requiring predetermined quantums of space, hygiene, food and supervision. Any individuality which they might display would be quirks, which upset the collective arrangements of the institution, and ought therefore not to be indulged. Instead of going to the considerable trouble of allowing residents to do things for themselves, like cooking and cleaning, all would be organised centrally. Communal dining and day rooms, and dormitories instead of bedrooms, would be preferred for the same reasons. Personal possessions, even personal clothing, would be seen as concessions to inefficiency. Wing and Brown[20] describe how,

> At one large hospital . . . large red C's are sewn prominently on the front of the oldest shirts (the C referred to the central stores). On more recent issues this mark is attached at the waist line. In the newest shirts it is relegated to the tail, but it is still present.

So, these attitudes still persist, even nowadays.

What one sees here is an attempt to maximise the economies of scale through specialisation — central kitchens, laundry, clothing stores, etc. But this involves denuding human beings of their social roles to an extent which would not be acceptable outside the institution, even in a technologically dominated society like ours. Hence the need to insulate life in the institution from outside values, and within that cocoon, to resocialise inmates into

9

acceptance of their new and impoverished life-style. This is the dynamic process which lies behind the phenomenon of the total institution, as it has been described by Erving Goffman (see the next chapter). Role dispossession means an attenuated personality arising out of a diminution in the stimulation and insight which different roles (and even a degree of role conflict) would normally have brought with them. It also causes a loss of points of contact with the environment, and a consequent reduction in involvement with it. Reduced personal awareness, and fewer transactions with the world outside oneself, can be expected as an outcome of these various deprivations.

This is depersonalisation, in the sense of a direct assault on the social personality of the inmate; but it also takes another related form. Warm interpersonal relationships, having some regard as they must do for the individuality of the people involved, can play little part in an institution organised in this way. So there is no emotional incentive for greater social participation by inmates either. Indeed all the evidence is that an emotionally unresponsive environment may cause individuals to fall back on their own narcissistic sources of emotional support, retreating still further into themselves. This is one of the conclusions to be drawn from the work of Bowlby, already referred to, but it is not confined to the infants whom he studied. Most of us will have had experience of behaving in this way when emotionally rebuffed, and we are talking about institution residents for whom such rebuffs are a permanent part of their lives.

One practical outcome of all this is the backwardness in speech noted among institution children.[21] Vocalisation appears to be the result of a maturational process, but speech arises out of a need and a desire to communicate, as well as the imitation of the speech of others around you. Children in institutions often live in rather unpromising conditions for the development of lively communication with others. Also because of the lack of personal relationships with the staff, they are forced to communicate mainly with other children, who provide poor models for imitation, and therefore for the development of vocabulary and speech skills.

In addition to depersonalisation in its two forms, it is argued that many residential establishments impose sensory deprivation on their residents. Techniques of interrogation during the Korean War involving the isolation of prisoners showed how dramatic the effects of such deprivation can be.[22] An experiment was carried out by Bexton and others,[23] in which students were confined to a bed, dressed in gloves and translucent goggles to reduce their input of visual and tactile stimuli, and left lying in silence except for the gentle, monotonous hum of a fan, which led to the victims of this bizarre treatment becoming hallucinated and temporarily disorientated, and losing their ability to concentrate and think clearly.

These were very extreme examples. The degree of sensory deprivation in any institution which our society would tolerate is going to be incomparably less than this. Nevertheless if one thinks about the restrictions on activity which are often imposed, the monotony of the regime, the uniformity of the physical environment, and the unstimulating nature of the institution's programme, some sensory deprivation does seem to be occurring in the more institutional of our residential homes. It is difficult to distinguish this form of deprivation from those designated above as depersonalisation; research in an infant home by Provence and Lipton[24] discovered a wide range of effects attributable to deprivation. These included poor visual discrimination, retarded locomotor abilities, constricted emotions, absence of the normal infant interest in their bodies and severe retardation of speech, of which at least the first two are probably due to sensory deprivation. For confirmation, White[25] set out to enrich the sensory experience of infants in institutions, by providing extra handling, changes in position (and therefore in visual field), and introducing colour and varied shapes to add visual interest to their surroundings. The result was a marked improvement in exploratory behaviour, expressed in the form of visually-directed reaching, and visual attention. Because of the importance of exploratory behaviour for later learning, a reduction in it which could be blamed on sensory deprivation in the institution would be a serious matter in any home for young children.

We have of course to be concerned also with other groups than babies, but because they are not very mobile, it is easier to standardise experimental conditions than it would be with older children or adults, and thus to isolate the factors involved. In the event, it seems that we have good reason to be concerned about sensory deprivation in residential homes of all kinds. The reduction in attention and outgoing interest which it brings with it seem very likely to contribute their own quota to the apathy and introversion which are so prominent among institutionalised individuals.

Finally there is the way in which the institution may cut off residents from the many social and leisure activities available to them outside. To some extent this is a natural consequence of life in a residential community. Company and social relations are to be found within the institution, and there is therefore little incentive to go to the trouble of joining in activities outside in order to make friends. The existence of the institution also represents a kind of psychological barrier to wider participation; it is not the same as going out in the evening from a family home. This effect may be reinforced by physical barriers: permitted hours, the need to get permission or a late key, an isolated rural setting or even a locked door. Self-containment like this may be attractive to total institutions of the traditional kind and to therapeutic communities, though of course for different reasons. The former would value the institutional convenience, and the latter the possibility of exercising more control over the formative experiences to which inmates were subjected.

Motives, however, in this as in so many other situations, are less important than consequences. Unless the loss of outside activities is compensated for by an active programme within the institution, both types of institution would end by stunting the development of their unfortunate residents. A prisoner in one long-term, maximum security prison, faced with the monotony and boredom of (literally) yawning tracts of unoccupied time, talked of having to learn to 'eat time'. Daydreaming is the commonest solution, in such a situation, whether in prisons, old people's homes, mental hospitals, mental deficiency institutions, etc.

All of these forms of social deprivation are interrelated. Dependency is a result of role dispossession, which in its disregard for the individual, leads to an impersonal regime, and an insensitivity to the individual need for stimulation. Failure to develop an adequate programme of activities arises from the same sources, and imposes not only its own very specific privations but also tends to reduce independence, role activity and personal relationships, as well as opportunities for sensory experience. It is not therefore surprising that their effects are similar. They seem to reinforce each other in producing the dependent and introverted response summed up in the word 'apathy', a word which is so often used to describe the institutionalised adaptation among inmates.

This effect of what Wing and Brown have called 'social poverty' in institutions has been well brought out by their research, which establishes an empirical relationship between social poverty in mental hospitals, and clinical deterioration in schizophrenic patients in those hospitals. The more institutional the regime, the more the patients manifest social withdrawal, flattening of feelings and speech impairment. Florid schizophrenic symptoms (delusion, hallucination, thought disorder, overactivity, eccentric behaviour) are less closely correlated with social poverty. One theory is that where escape through withdrawal is not encouraged by the unsocialising effect of an institutional environment, the schizophrenic will react to stress by producing florid symptoms.[26] One could not have a better example of the Scylla and Charybdis between which the institution has to try to steer: on the one hand avoiding the dead hand of social poverty, and on the other hand protecting the resident from excessive pressures, which he is at present unable to tolerate.

The schizophrenic patient's withdrawal in an impoverished institutional environment is only an extreme example of the development we have witnessed among other kinds of residents in similar residential climates. But in admitting as they do that biological factors may also play a part in determining the outcome with their schizophrenics, Wing and Brown remind us of the importance of personal vulnerability. Individual differences may have some share in determining whether or not inmates will in fact react to social poverty by a decline into institutionalised dependence and apathy in other kinds of home also.

If institutionalisation is to be avoided, social workers have to prevent social poverty in its various forms from spreading in their homes. Assuming that this can be done, do we have to retreat so completely from the idea of the residential institution? Is there not some value in total care of the sort which can only be provided under residential conditions? Has the pendulum not once more swung too far? Yet the case for residential care still has to be elucidated. We have to give more attention than we have in the past to the role which we intend it to perform within the structure of our social services.

In the past institutions for particular groups emerged one by one, simply to meet a felt need to dispose tidily and cheaply of our unwanted fellow-citizens. They were social dustbins, and as such, their aims were containment, combined with cheapness and ease of administration. Hence the rigorously disciplined barracks of the nineteenth century. Since then ideologies of care and treatment have been imposed on them, aims which they were neither built nor organised to realise. Moreover, our sociological naivety caused us to try to achieve through residential care, aims which they could not realise no matter how modern their buildings or their methods. Only now are we beginning to understand that some social work objectives can only be frustrated if attempted away from the normal community and within the four walls of an institution. The question confronting us now is not whether the residential institution still has a role to play, but what that role is; when it should be brought into play and with what kinds of client, and above all what methods it must use if it is to attain its objectives, and avoid institutionalisation. These are the questions which this book seeks to explore.

Chapter two

Regimes

The regime of an institution is the way in which it is governed — the overall trends in the way in which it is run. Thus it may be on the one hand 'strict' or on the other hand 'permissive'. It may concentrate on inculcating good habits in its inmates by insisting on conformity to certain rules of good behaviour, or it may operate on the basis of more complex theories of human behaviour derived from Freudian or other schools of psychology. Relations between staff and inmates may be formal and distant, or casual and warm. The institution may keep its members (often staff as well as inmates) rigidly apart from the surrounding community, or encourage maximum interaction between the two. It may operate on a mass-handling basis (like the 'barracks' institutions referred to in the previous chapter) or on the individualised basis possible only in a small establishment. And so on.

Although any particular regime consists of a constellation of such characteristics as these, they are not normally a random collection. They tend to be congruent with one another in the sense of reflecting a common underlying philosophy. Thus strictness, impersonality, habit-training and large-group methods often go together, and reinforce each other. Habit-training can be carried out *en masse*, and requires strict enforcement, and a degree of emotional detachment.

The regime, in the sense of an overall pattern, has more importance than anything else for the impact which an institution has on those who live in it. A particular innovation may be introduced into the programme with the aim of ameliorating some of the effects of the regime, but unless it actually changes the regime it cannot usually expect to produce the desired results. Either its effects will be nullified by the more all-pervasive and many-faceted influences emanating from the regime, or it will tend to accommodate itself to that overall design, while often still adhering formally to its own objectives which in practice it has either given up, or drastically re-interpreted. An example of this is the role of the medical officer in the prison. He has a professional commitment to the health of his prison patients, but is eventually caught up in the overall containment philosophy of the prison, and is quicker to see, and harder on possible 'malingerers' than he would be with his patients in private practice. As Dr R. R. Prewer, a Principal Medical Officer with almost forty years' service in prisons, frankly admits:[1] 'One thing is quite certain, and that is that Medicine is going to play a larger and larger part in both the treatment and control of those offenders who come into penal institutions'; and in case there might be any doubt about his meaning, he concludes, 'treatment and control are merely two sides of the same coin'.

One must not present too monistic a picture of a regime. It usually includes at least four separate social systems each enforcing different patterns of social behaviour, *viz.* the official prescription, a staff society, an inmate society, and an area of common ground. Nevertheless there is an internal consistency in such a regime: its differing constituent parts have a mutually supportive relationship. Each is a precondition for the existence of the others. There was, after all, a good deal of truth in George Bernard Shaw's remark that it was the existence of prostitution which made Christian marriage possible. In the same way, the discharge and legitimation of staff or inmate dissatisfaction, within these subcultures, may be part of the balance which enables the regime itself to survive. This is a matter which will be taken up in more detail later.

If genuine incompatibilities do exist within the institution, say a substantial group of staff who reject the regime and are in a position to pursue their own ideas in their work, in defiance of the 'official line', then the result may be that neither policy is being effectively realised. One then has a *ritualised* institution, performing certain motions, and paying lip-service to the attainment of certain objectives, but unable to give reality to either. The regime appears to remain intact, but it is little more than an empty shell.

All of which implies that regimes are designed in the way they are as a means to the realisation of particular aims. The nature of these goals is not however always clear. Sometimes a number of conflicting objectives may be espoused by the institution — though the incompatibility may not always be acknowledged or even understood. One may then find one aim being realised at the expense of the other (to which lip-service nevertheless continues to be paid), or the attempt to realise both may frustrate them both. An example is using an old people's home as both a means of relieving relatives of the burden of their old folks, and providing proper social care for them. The latter calls for a close contact to be maintained between

15

the elderly clients and their families in order to keep their interest active and the emotions and faculties alive. However, the old people's home is only too convenient as a repository for an incubus like an aged father or mother, and so visits and other contacts often gradually fade out. It is not uncommon then for the institution to concentrate on the physical care and comfort of the deserted old person, and on offering him such emotional sustenance as the staff and fellow-inmates can provide. The satisfaction of his needs has been curtailed in the interest of the institution's 'repository function'.

Nor is the objective to which the institution lays claim necessarily that at which it is actually aiming, by the regime which it adopts. Robert Merton[2] distinguishes usefully here between manifest and latent functions — 'between conscious motivations for social behaviour and its objective consequences'. As already hinted, a review of residential care suggests that although a variety of fine-sounding justifications have been given for placing people in institutions, the purpose above all others which they have been used to serve has been that of a repository — a *cordon sanitaire* behind which can be secluded fellow-citizens who might otherwise be a cause of anxiety to us.

Because this was the primary task of nineteenth-century institutions, their regimes took the form they did. Goffman[3] has characterised them as 'total institutions', total in the sense of being institutions in which all the activities of their inmates are undertaken — in contrast to non-institutional life, in which 'the individual tends to sleep, play and work in different places, with different co-participants, under different authorities, and without an overall rational plan'. Their all-inclusive nature necessarily means that inmates are withdrawn from normal roles and social interaction; seclusiveness becomes their defining feature. All else about them follows from this. In particular, inmates on reception have to be detached from their pre-institutional roles and identifications, and have to be reshaped to enable them to adjust to the life-style of a total institution. Because these practices represent an attempt to change the inmate's whole view of his personal identity by a series of direct onslaughts, Goffman speaks of them as 'mortifications of self'.

Restrictions are placed on the contacts of inmates with the outside world, through letters, visits, etc., presumably to eliminate any social influences which might compete with the institution in its efforts to capture them. Personal belongings from outside are taken away and stored against the day of release. Outside clothing with all its importance for the individual's physical self-image is replaced by institution garb, so that he literally must see himself as an inmate. His name is replaced by some institution label — often a number. All of these changes have great significance for the person's self-concept: what he owns, wears and calls himself are all part of his own individuality as he sees it. So to change them, to give them an institutional character, is to travel part of the way towards giving him an institutional identity.

The next stage is often an 'obedience test' designed to ensure his submission to institutional authority quite early on in his residence there. Goffman presents a telling example from Behan's *Borstal Boy* in which a recalcitrant Behan, refusing to defer to the staff of his borstal, is eventually brought to heel by physical force. Privacy for sleeping and the performance of intimate personal functions is lost, eliminating still more of the 'separateness' which militates against the absorption of a person in an institutional regime. Even his rationality is subverted; any opposition to the regime being confronted by a process which Goffman calls 'looping' — 'explaining away' his opposition to what was happening to him as merely another manifestation of the problem which brought him into the institution in the first place. Thus a mental patient's rejection of a treatment on the grounds that he disliked it might be seen as being due instead to a desire not to recover from his mental illness, because if he did recover he would be faced once again by the problems of adjustment which he had attempted to avoid by means of his illness in the first place.

Finally there is the all-pervasive regimentation of the resident, extending often to control over his most trivial acts. The preceding 'mortification' processes are both a means of detaching an individual from this past, and of inculcating in him the attitudes which will fit him for his future in the institution. The regimentation of his life there also performs a dual function: it not only represents a convenient way of running the establishment, but also a continual process of re-education for 'fitting-in', both through the habits engendered in inmates by the enforced repetition of certain acts, and by the operation of the customary system of rewards and punishments. Even the institution newspaper, ward social, visiting choir and so on help to centre the attention of inmates on the life of the institution rather than on the outside world, thus playing their part in helping it to fulfil its secluding function.

That this is the primary function of the institution seems clear from Goffman's analysis. If further proof were needed, it is to be found in the way in which the management of an institution are held to account if any breach of seclusion occurs. Thus there is an outcry if (whether intended or not) mental patients exhibiting eccentric behaviour are seen on the street, or too many escapes occur from prisons. In physical medicine such complaints have to do with sending hospital patients home 'too soon', i.e. in such a way as to impose risk on them, or trouble or embarrassment to their relatives. And although Goffman does not make this point, inmates of institutions are expected to be 'contained' not only by being physically incarcerated, but also by having their behaviour within, restrained, so that echoes of what was happening inside did not escape to trouble the general public outside.

This second aspect of the 'seclusion function' is one of the reasons for the regimentation referred to. It is also adopted, however, because of the need to 'manage the daily activity of a large number of people in a restricted space with a small expenditure of resources'. One might go further and say that the total institution as such, given its basic function of seclusion, provides a means by which one can thus systematise the management of a large number of people and so save space and resources. In other words a regime necessary for achieving the segregation of inmates is also a regime in which economies for the mass-processing of people can be realised.

Goffman recognises that this picture may be overdrawn. He points to the way in which the outside world can influence what goes on in the institution and vice versa. He also talks about 'secondary adjustments' by which inmates can escape into undercover informal relationships with each other, which can soften the socialising rigour of the institution. Nevertheless one is left with the impression that these breaches in the regime are relatively unimportant. It is difficult to square this view of the regime as a largely inexorable and inescapable machine for processing people, with his contention that the effects of this powerful process of socialisation do not last long after the individual is discharged. In particular the so-called 'secondary adjustments' are probably less secondary, and of much greater importance than he seems to believe. Goffman (rather surprisingly for a symbolic interactionist) is guilty of devoting too much attention to the formal aspects of the life of the institution at the expense of the informal.

What is in question here is not only the role of what is sometimes called the 'inmate subculture'. This aspect of the residential community has justifiably received a good deal of attention from students of institutions in the past. What has not always been acknowledged is the parallel importance of the informal 'staff sub-culture'; recent researches suggest that this may be even stronger than that of the inmates.

Goffman argues that under the conditions of the total institution, it is impossible for inmates to keep secrets from the authorities for very long — hence no doubt the subordinate role assigned by him to secondary adjustments. Gresham Sykes[4] is nearer to the mark in saying that total control by the staff, even in a prison, where one might expect it to be easiest, is impossible to achieve. The staff may therefore get to know what is going on, but be in no position to compel conformity. All they can do is bargain for it, and long-term inmates have almost as much stake in peace and quiet as the staff. Constant upheavals provoking frequent disciplinary measures are to nobody's advantage. Out of this situation emerges the so-called 'custodial compromise',[5] in which an implicit agreement is reached between inmates and front-line staff that no action will be taken to insist on strict adherence to the rules, so long as superficial conformity is maintained. On the inmate side this means that in exchange for support for the fabric of order in the institution a degree of indulgence is granted to the undercover inmate subculture.

Of course there is .a limit to what could be tolerated, and experienced inmates are well aware of this. Nevertheless this hidden inmate society does come to present a striking contrast to the institution as the public knows it, assuming a compensatory role of the kind implied by Goffman's concept of 'secondary adjustments'. Sykes similarly sees the inmate society of the prison as compensating for the 'pains of imprisonment'. This mirror-image aspect only fails to become a contraculture because of the unspoken agreement reached between staff and inmates about the fundamental basis of solidarity in the institution.

The extent to which this subverts the *official* aims of the institution calls for closer examination. It is often pointed out that while the 'total institution' features of a prison account for its institutionalising effects on inmates, their subjection to the pressures from the inmate subculture often cause them also to be 'criminalised'. These two effects together constitute the complex and corrupting process which Clemmer[6] calls 'prisonisation'. In this way the inmate society seems to be achieving ends which are directly contrary to those of the prison authorities. When evaluated in the light of the cynicism of front-line staff, the aims of the prisoner subculture are seen as not so very divergent from the expectations of the prison officers. In tolerating an inmate subculture, prison officers are, it seems, at the same time adjusting their ideas about the aims of the prison in a realistic fashion.

Most has been written about the inmate underworld in prisons. A few such studies have been concerned with correctional schools.[7] The phenomenon is probably most fully developed in penal institutions. This is only to be expected. As the norms of criminals will be so much more divergent from the official norms of the institution, they will, in being required to adapt, have more to compensate for. There has been some debate between penologists as to whether the anti-social norms of the prisoner subculture do arise as Sykes suggested, as a way of relieving some of the 'pains of imprisonment', or whether they are the natural result of bringing together in a prison men with a prior attachment to anti-social norms.[8] The truth is probably that both are involved.

A similar analysis applies to other than prisoner groups. It is age and sometimes social class which mark out the inmates of a children's or old people's home from those who run the institution, and this determines how and to what extent the former must find compensation in their own hidden society. Where delinquency is added, as in a correctional school, differences are sharpened, and the inmate subculture strengthened accordingly.[9] Mental hospital patients, at least in the less acute wards, also seem to have a fairly active informal inmate society of this kind,[10] which in Goffman's terminology enables them to 'make our' in the institution.

The institutionalising effects emerging from the overworld of the residential establishment and the contaminating (in penal institutions, 'criminalising') effects of the underworld, being compensatory to each other, tend to be alternatives. Where one is strong, the other is weak. It is probably the inability of old people to summon the vigour required for the development of a very active inmate culture which accounts for the predominantly institutionalising effect which old people's homes have. Similarly, but because of limitations of understanding, in institutions for the mentally subnormal — or for infants!

It remains to discuss the staff subculture. Although there must be implicit understandings uniting all staff working in institutions, the attitudes which really matter are those of what has been called the 'front-line staff', those involved in direct day-to-day contact with residents. It is this group who have most need for a 'custodial compromise', without which work would become impossible. It is therefore at this level that the custodial compromise emerges. As Goffman points out this group of staff tend to be the most permanent element in the institution's population. Inmates come and go, and staff who are promoted are often, as a result, moved elsewhere. Quite apart therefore from the salience given to their ideas by the fact that they *are* the front-line staff so that any policy has to be given flesh and blood by them, this permanence of theirs means that it is their ideas which will persist against the influences from transitory figures like superintendents and others.

As with inmates, those ideas will be determined partly by the personal characteristics and previous experience of staff, and partly by the opportunities and deprivations presented to them by the job. How and from what groups staff are selected is crucial for the first of these. In practice certain kinds of institution which have low status, such as institutions for the infirm elderly or for subnormals, tend to have to take whatever staff they can get. Although there are exceptions these will often themselves be persons of low status who have taken these less desirable jobs *faute de mieux*. It is a sombre reflection on our attitudes to both aged and black people that a disproportionate number of black nurses are often found in geriatric wards.

Apart from this kind of factor, staff will be selected according to the prevailing view of what the particular kind of institution should be achieving, and therefore what the staff should be capable of. Where, as is so often the case, the containment of the behaviour of inmates is ranked high among the institution's aims, staff will be selected with their ability to maintain discipline well to the fore. Such staff can then represent a major source of informal resistance to any later attempt to move away from the total-institution pattern.

The other effect on staff norms, that produced by the nature of the job, is up to a point quite straightforward. Prison staff are going to be more apprehensive and punitive than staff of a children's home because criminals are seen as dangerous, while children tend to evoke quasi-parental feelings in those who look after them. Where, as in the case of the mentally subnormal or the very aged, the inmate group is incapable of putting up much resistance; they are more likely to be organised for the convenience of the staff, losing much of their individuality in the process. These being also the conditions in which the inmate society is weakest, tend to be the most fertile soil for the growth of institutionalisation.

There are, however, subtler aspects in the staff response to their task. Menzies[11] shows how even the official norms of the nursing profession (norms about professional detachment, etc.) arise as means by which the staff are protected from the emotional stresses of involvement with death and suffering, or the temptations arising from intimate physical association with patients. This kind of study is still in its infancy, but there are some obvious possibilities for further work along these lines. Much depends on methods of selecting staff, but it may be that some of the punitive behaviour which some staff manifest in those institutions which do not have great appeal to potential employees (e.g. prisons, geriatric or subnormality institutions) may be the result of self-justificatory behaviour on the part of the staff of such places, who are often, as we have seen, the less successful. If you have not been very successful yourself, it is a relief to exercise power over others, compare yourself favourably with them, or even deflect your resentment at your failure on to them — all accompanied of course by appropriate rationalisations.

Relations between different levels of staff are also important in the total picture. As already suggested there may be considerable barriers to communication between them. Lower-level staff may protect their own subculture from their superiors as carefully as do inmates from them, presenting, like the inmates, an anxiety-allaying surface impression of the situations with which they are dealing. And this secret world, like that of inmates, probably also fulfils the function of providing them with satisfactions which the uncompensated rule of their employers would withhold from them.

The regime then is more than the official system of rules and practices. The ramifications of the official system are widespread, and any realistic attempt to understand how an institution works, and what effects it has on both inmates and staff must take them into account. As must any attempt to provide some alternative to the traditional total institution. Behind what follows is a belief in the possibility of doing this. And an essential precondition is the displacement of the latent 'repository' aim, by making a reality of those more defensible institutional aims to which only lip-service has been paid in the past.

In attempting this in any particular institution, the first struggle will be with the past. The previous regime existed because there was a public demand for it; it catered for the public's need to 'sweep its problems under the carpet'. Any proposals for change are therefore going to meet with a very mixed reception. As in the past there will be plenty of support for high-sounding ideals, but when it is proposed to put these into operation, the reformer will be made only too well aware that the results are to be watched very closely and critically. In the face of such pressure innovations are often watered-down, on the ground that an adverse public opinion might be aroused by any early failures, and abort the changes from the beginning. Such timidity is not cost-free; the price is often paid in the form of disillusionment on the part of the potential beneficiaries of the new policy. A good example is the attempt to get men out of prison by means of parole. In its early days the Parole Board adopted a very cautious policy, awarding parole in only a relatively few, fairly safe cases, precisely for fear that if many parole break-downs occurred they would cause the public to lose confidence in parole as such, thus hampering its further development. This did not happen, but nobody who knows British prisons could be in any doubt about the widespread cynicism about parole this policy has engendered among prisoners. Few, even among those who apply for parole, believe that they have any chance of getting it.[12]

As far as the reform of regimes is concerned there is another danger. As pointed out earlier, small changes have little chance of succeeding against the general drift of a regime. They tend to be assimilated: to be modified so that they support rather than run counter to the *status quo*. An example of this is the way in which psychiatrists in some mental hospitals become part of the containment machinery, using drugs instead of physical restraints it is true, but still seeing the tranquillising of patients as an important part of their role. It would of course be an essential requirement for the realisation of the repository role of a mental hospital. Marginal changes in regimes then will not be effective; only changes which actually shift the centre of gravity of an institution can expect to be so.

Apart from conservative pressures from the public, the would-be reformer will have to contend with resistance from the staff, appointed under the old order presumably because their backgrounds and personalities suited the institution as it had been heretofore. In addition change means disturbing the existing equilibrium within the institution. However desirable change may be on other grounds, it does involve staff in giving up a safe and intelligible pattern of work, and plunging into the unknown. And it should be remembered that any new policy would have to be implemented through the agency of those very staff. The chief danger is not grumbling, and dissatisfaction, or even revolt on their part; often such manifestations of dissent can be dealt with by a resolute administration which is clear about its objectives. The greater threat comes from the ability of front-line staff to administer a policy in such a way as to preserve all its forms but change its essential character.

All of this is merely an instance of the general problem of bringing about social change, which is the core of the social work task. Social workers are accustomed to dealing with resistance to change from casework clients, and accept that it is the existence of such resistance which provides the *raison d'être* for casework method. Resistance to changes of regime in institutions could easily come to be seen as something outside of social work: an expression of bloody-mindedness which must be thrust aside so that the real social work can proceed. In fact if it is to be successfully dealt with, it must be approached with professional understanding and skill of a high order. More will be said about this.

Regimes will be related to the needs which they are intended to satisfy. What consequences does this have for the way in which institutions operate? A basic distinction needs to be made between needs for short-term and long-term care. The former is required in two kinds of instance. The first is where the need for temporary care arises out of an emergency in the home of say a mental patient, an old person or a child. The relative or other person usually responsible has to go into hospital or needs a holiday, or even simply needs a rest from the stresses of looking after the client. The kind of care required in such cases is one which will not in any way disturb the client's present relationships or mode of adjustment, but will simply provide him with a kind of holiday experience. It may be possible to use the opportunity to make up some of the minor deficiencies in his existing life-style, by expanding the range of his interests as by introducing him to hobbies, etc. On the whole, however, in such cases it is assumed either by the client or the person responsible for him that no rehabilitative action is expected. Indeed, far from being required, any important change in him might simply have the effect of making him less well-adjusted to his permanent environment when he returns to it after his 'holiday break'. The emphasis then would be on temporary relationships and continuity of life-style.

The other major role for the short-stay institution will be as a 'transitional community'[13] seeking to bring about changes in clients. This is the institution as an agency of rehabilitation. Its clientele might be delinquents or criminals, people who are mentally or physically ill, children in need of special educational treatment and so on. The idea that rehabilitation requires short-term institutions is a break with traditional thinking, which was to the effect that the longer clients stayed, the more likely were they to be influenced by the institution. The new conception is partly a result of new technical developments in medicine, psychiatry and even social work by which people can be brought quickly to a state at which they can function outside the institution. A most striking example of this is in the use of drugs for the control of symptoms in cases of schizophrenia.

However, as we have seen in Chapter 1, there has also been a change in the climate of opinion, as the effect of long-term residence in institutions has been better understood. Rehabilitation is a form of social training or 'socialisation', and arises out of a complex interaction between a person and his total social environment. As we have seen, to undergo that experience within a total institution merely adapts the client to the institution, and actually damages his accommodation to normal outside society. Rehabilitation is clearly best undertaken in that outside society where the interactions involved will be more relevant to the kind of life he is expected to lead afterwards. So if his rehabilitation requires a spell in an institution, it is important that it should be short. And this carries with it the corollary that the process of rehabilitation in the institution will be intensive. The regime must be a kind of 'forcing-house' for change, often with a further implication that the process will continue in some way into the immediate post-institution life of the client.

Where then does long-term care fit in, if at all? Three major categories of care are to be distinguished — the institution as an asylum, as a means of protecting the public, and as a means for the nurture of children.

The word 'asylum' is being used in its proper meaning of a haven, rather than in the pejorative sense in which it has common currency. Some old people, chronically sick, or mentally or physically handicapped persons, etc. who are unable to cope by themselves and have nobody either willing or able to take care of them, usually need such a haven where they can enjoy, for fairly lengthy periods, possibly for their lifetimes, the social, emotional, intellectual and physical conditions normally provided by a good family home. The total institution cannot provide such conditions. Nor incidentally can institutions based on a medical model. It is regrettable that so many institutions for long-term residents (a particular case is that of the institution for the mentally handicapped) have been defined as hospitals and handed over to the medical professions, when their medical needs are so marginal, capable of being met in the same way as those of residents of other institutions by the ordinary provisions of the National Health Service. Their need is only to a limited extent for some form of rehabilitation; they are long-term residents whose condition it is hoped can be maintained at a stable level. They want the comforts of a good home, and enough stimulation to prevent deterioration, rather than treatment. And that is inconsistent with the atmosphere of a hospital, with its white coats, clinical atmosphere, and rigid hierarchies.

The reference to treatment is to medical treatment. It does not follow that no behavioural or social progress will be possible in these cases. The history of the treatment of spastics shows that professional pessimism can sometimes be confounded by enthusiasts who refuse to give up. Activity lost by old people as a result of living alone or under bad environmental conditions can be regained if the regime is such as to make it more worthwhile and more manageable. Withdrawal from social relationships can be reversed if such relationships are available and attractive. Handicapped residents, no matter how limited their physical or mental powers, can be trained to do some things for themselves. Besides, the best form of defence against deterioration is the social climate produced in a home by the impetus towards effecting positive improvement in clients. How much pressure of this kind is desirable is a matter of judgment. The institution is primarily a haven. To be constantly calling for improvement from old people who really want to enjoy a little peace and quiet would be insensitive and cruel.

The other danger for the long-term institution is that it will eventually deteriorate into a total institution of the traditional kind. Administrative efficiency and staff convenience alike tend to lead to centralised organisation with its mass methods and impersonality. The centralised kitchen, laundry, cleaning service, have obvious organisational advantages. By comparison, leaving these things to be done for themselves by inmates (even with supervision) is untidy and wasteful. There is also a temptation to restrict the movements of residents outside the institution. This enables their safety to be better ensured, as well as making it possible to control their contacts with the neighbouring community. But it is also, as we have seen, a way of impoverishing their social personalities. Because they may have to spend the rest of their lives in the institution is no justification for restricting the range of their satisfactions and responses in this way. Children in an institution for the mentally handicapped were encouraged to take part-time jobs delivering newspapers in the neighbourhood, thus both earning money and enjoying worthwhile new experiences.[14] Occasionally things went awry. A subnormal boy would become confused by the problems of organising his deliveries and dumping all the newspapers on a doorstep would run home to the institution. At such times there would be pressure to break off the experiment. One has to make contingency plans to meet these situations when they occur, but ought not to try to prevent them simply by withdrawing back into one's shell.

Such tendencies are less likely to arise in small than in large institutions, because personal involvement is then unavoidable, arousing sympathy and understanding; and also because the advantages of overorganising people are fewer, and therefore less of a temptation. There is also much to be said for hostel-type institutions from which residents can go out to work or for recreation. The day centre where people live at home, but come in daily for work, training or treatment is another variant.

The long-term institution designed for the protection of the public will generally be a prison. In the past we have had preventive detention, and at the present time we have extended sentences. They represent a clear breach of traditional ideas about justice: the individual is not being incarcerated solely as a punishment for what he has done. The retributive or 'deserved' punishment for his crime would have been a shorter one. But in the interest of the public it has been decided that he must be locked away for a longer period. The implication from this is that his imprisonment must not be any more uncomfortable for him than is absolutely necessary for achieving the aim of containing him effectively. But simply making him comfortable is not enough; one day he will be returned to the community and we must at least ensure that he is not institutionalised by his sentence and thus made less capable of surviving outside. And as we have seen there is the further danger, in a penal institution, of his being criminalised by the contacts he makes within the inmate underworld.

Indeed as with the asylum one should go further even in the

preventive institution, and aim at rehabilitation. It is a difficult setting within which to essay this, but we certainly do not as yet know enough about human nature to justify us in writing-off anybody. And as we have seen one advantage of setting the institution a correctional target is that it introduces a vitalising element into the regime which will act as an antidote to any institutionalising tendency. Perhaps one cannot prevent the institution from doing harm without trying to make it do some good. This could be the fallacy in the views of Sir Rupert Cross[15] and others, who see little point in trying to do more than prevent the deterioration of prisoners. Although similarities between the asylum and the institution for the protection of the public may be obscured by deterrent and punitive feelings about criminals, they have a good deal in common. So much of what has been said about ways of organising the former apply also to the latter.

The nurturant institution is attempting to do something which is normally the task of the family, and which experience suggests the family (in one of its many forms) does best. The later development of the kibbutzim of Israel, with the increasing involvement of parents,[16] has tended only to confirm this. For this purpose, then, the institution is usually second-best, and will be better the more closely it resembles the family. Although smallness and openness therefore go without saying, the first essential is staff who understand and can relate to children, and who get enough satisfaction themselves out of the relationship to make them want to give something of themselves in return. All social work relationships transcend the professional, 'paid-for' association, by the presence within them of this emotional factor; but love, which cannot be bought, is such a vital element in the healthy development of children that it must loom larger here than elsewhere. Professional casework was right in calling attention to what the psychoanalysts call the counter-transference:[17] such a degree of emotional dependence by social workers on their clients as to disable them from helping, or even causing them to exploit clients emotionally to satisfy their own needs. However, this is no justification for detachment. Social work means being part of a symbiotic process with your clients, and nowhere more so than in work with children.

Chapter three

Justifications

It is one thing to define the objectives of a regime in broad terms, as in the last chapter. It is quite another to convert these generalisations about nurture, change, shelter, containment and temporary shelter into actual interventions in people's lives. At this point the question of justification is bound to arise: what right do we have to disturb people's life-styles and relationships, especially in the drastic way that residential placement entails? There is no problem if it is assumed, as it has so often been in the past, that dominant cultural norms are always right. Anybody who does not fit in is then fair game. His very non-conformity is clear evidence that he is in the wrong, and ought to be subjected to some remedial action in order to bring him into line. Even this, as an approach through 'treatment', would have been seen at one time as a concession. A generation earlier, the deviant would have been coerced into capitulation by punishment or the threat of it.

Whether subjected to the 'hard sell' of compulsion, or the 'soft sell' of persuasion and casework, such a client could easily be having a vital decision taken out of his hands. On the other hand the word 'client' properly implies someone who employs a professional (in this case a social worker) in order to try to realise his, the client's, own aims; and professional social work has adopted the concept of the client in this sense. This would seem to make it possible for the social worker to play a radical part in emancipating our deviants, though to see him in this light is to fail to recognise the extent to which he is himself constrained by his own position within the social structure.

Social workers are employed either by government (or local government) or by voluntary welfare organisations. All of these bodies have their own axes to grind, and employ social workers to that end. Thus the state wishes to eliminate 'social problems', in the sense of breaches of the prevailing norms of behaviour. Some of these social problems consist of lawbreaking, while others involve the flouting of conventional standards of morality, cleanliness, thrift, orderliness, etc. The voluntary agencies, as themselves products of the prevailing ethos of the society, usually subscribe to these general ideals, but also have more specific aims in mind. Many of them, for example, originated from particular religious denominations, which not only gives a special moral or even theological coloration to how they approach clients and look on their behaviour, but also helps to determine their objectives. Concepts like the Christian family and even Christian observance loom large in what they expect of their clients.

It is in order to realise ends of these kinds that social workers are employed. For them to seek instead to pursue ends designated for them by their clients, who by definition are subject to the ministrations of social workers precisely because they have rejected or been unable to meet prevailing norms, would be to run counter to the aims and purposes of their employers, and would receive short shrift from the latter. In the past there has been in any case little conflict of this kind because the people recruited for social work have themselves been in the main committed to the standards expressed by their agencies. They have come from the respectable working, and lower middle classes, who, in seeking to better themselves by hard work, saving, education and an orderly way of life, reflect most closely the dominant cultural norms which social workers are expected to work to sustain. Recruits to voluntary agencies often similarly support the special orientations of their organisations. For example, the staffs of organisations with a religious basis usually have a Christian commitment.

Nevertheless they are faced with a dilemma. On the one hand they are constrained by their agencies to and have also a personal preference for a particular set of goals. Their responsibilities to their employers are further underlined by traditional social work doctrine which lays stress on the importance of working within the limits laid down by the agency — the so-called 'agency function'[1] of the social worker. On the other hand the idea of a client-worker relationship would lead in the opposite direction, and this also has been legitimised in social work theory by the importance attached to client self-determination.[2]

Is there any real dilemma here? Surely there is broad agreement in our society between all classes as to what makes for the 'good life' and the 'good society'. Some sociologists, who adopt what is known as a consensus view of society, would argue that this is the case. A case in point is David Matza[3] who contends that criminals do feel guilty about their offences, and try to make excuses for themselves

— the so-called 'techniques of neutralisation'. The same consensus view is implicit in the writings of other sociologists from Durkheim to Talcott Parsons and Robert Merton.

An alternative, conflict, viewpoint is that there are within society a number of subgroups, which have enough in common with one another to form what may be called 'subcultures', able to co-exist with one another, but nevertheless differing in their beliefs in ways which cause the behaviour of the subgroups to differ radically.[4] These subgroups may be social classes, particular local neighbourhoods, ethnic subgroups (immigrants as against the indigenous population, for example). But they do not differ only in their beliefs; they differ also in social power, so that the more powerful are able to incorporate their ideas in the law and the penumbra of custom and convention, which together make up what has been referred to earlier as the dominant value system of the society. G. B. Vold, though referring to this process only as it affects the law, puts it very well: 'In other words, the whole process of law-making, law-breaking and law enforcement becomes a direct reflection of deep-seated and fundamental conflicts between interest groups and their more general struggle for the control of the police power of the state.'[5] Such ideas represent a continuing theme in the writings of the marxists, and appear in another form in the work of the German sociologist Georg Simmel.[6]

There are also individual forms of non-conformity. There have always been eccentrics, and some of these odd-men-out have proved in the end to see further and more clearly than the masses who derided them. Few of them will eventually assume the historical significance of a Socrates, a Jesus Christ or a Galileo; most will indeed be cranks or even criminals. Nevertheless, as John Stuart Mill states so eloquently in his *Essay on Liberty*, the suppression of non-conformity, quite apart from any value one attaches to freedom of action for its own sake, does involve a social cost in a loss of creativity and a reduction of the number of growing-points within the society. Nor does democracy provide a justification. As Mill so clearly saw, for a majority to impose its beliefs on a minority is still tyranny.

Ultimately, however, it is the possession of power which determines whose beliefs will prevail. If the fathers of the American revolution had lost their struggle with George III they would have been stigmatised as traitors; in the event they became national heroes. And this illustrates the social worker's moral predicament: how to reconcile his acceptance of the judgments of those with power, with the slight possibility that his clients might have right on their side. In any case they are his clients, and are also entitled as free men, to make their own mistakes. Squaring the circle, we are told, is impossible. Professional social work seems to have achieved this miracle, resolving its uncertainties by means of what might be called the 'sickness assumption'.[7]

Deviance from the accepted standards of behaviour is due, we are told, to either personal or social sickness. The client may be the victim of a personal psychological disturbance of which deviance is merely a symptom, or of faulty attitudes. Or he may be living in a socially 'diseased' local neighbourhood which evokes difficult or anti-social behaviour from him. In seeking to change his behaviour, either through personal casework with him or community work to change attitudes in his locality, the social worker is (although the client may not at first realise it) on his side. He is merely trying to cure him of his social sickness. Deviance is equated with abnormality; in removing one, one is providing a remedy for the other, enabling the social worker to be at one and the same time, both a faithful servant of the *status quo* and of his client.

This justification is constantly being used when residential placement is proposed. Magistrates send children to correctional schools 'for their own good'. Mentally retarded persons need the protection and specialised treatment available to them in the institution. The reality of what happens in many such establishments hardly matches up to these claims, whereas the revulsion and inconvenience felt by the general population at having such people about the streets is clear enough.

When once in the institution the same justification continues to hold sway. Controlling the behaviour of inmates is good for them because they thus become habituated to good behaviour, and so are changed permanently for the better. This is of course the total institution at work, adapting its inmates to its convenience in the way described in earlier chapters. It shows how purely institutional imperatives begin to operate, side by side with other motives for containment which have a broader origin outside the institution. And both adopt the same spurious guise of being for the client's benefit. Another example of this kind is the way in which old people are restricted in what they are allowed to do for themselves in a home, ostensibly in order to protect them from possible accident, or from the anxiety and bother of cooking their own meals or doing their own washing. It is presumably coincidental that centralising such provision also makes it very much easier to run the home.

Very close to this are policies arising out of the more personal needs of staff in homes. Residential work is admittedly emotionally demanding. Staff are doing work which closely resembles core roles within the family, arousing within them the feelings they have about their own families. Thus childless spinsters (or bachelors) are tempted to give special attention amounting to favouritism to certain

31

attractive children in the home in which they work, and justify it on the grounds of the children's special need. Of course if such provision could be made for all the children in the home (for all will have such needs), good rather than harm would ensue. The fact that this is not what happens shows that this is not why it is done. Jealousies among residential staffs are also common, and readily understood when seen as analogous to sibling rivalry within the family.

An even more widespread example of the way in which the personal needs of staff lead to policies which are then rationalised as in the interests of residents, is to be found in the maintenance of firm discipline in the home. This is often as much for the peace of mind of the staff, as because of the public demand for containment. This, like favouritism, or jealousy between parental figures, is not unknown also in ordinary family situations. People who vent their rage or insecurity on their uncomprehending old folks, or who feel that their own tenuous self-control is threatened when their children misbehave, so that they must suppress that behaviour at once, will often also say that it is all for their victim's 'own good'.

In the language of the last chapter, we have to get behind the bogus manifest to the real but latent reasons for what we do in institutions, and we shall then find ourselves back with the dilemma between the interest of client and of society from which the 'sickness assumption' was supposed to rescue us. To meet this problem current social work theory has evolved the idea of a 'contract'[8] between client and social worker. This acknowledges that they may sometimes have different aims in mind, but assumes that they can reach a *modus vivendi* — agreement about the objectives to be sought in their relationship with one another. The term 'contract' is thus used in social work in an entirely analogous way to that in which it is used in commerce: as an agreement freely entered into by all parties because they feel it is to their mutual benefit. It implies, as far as social work is concerned, that from the outset the social worker will keep the client informed about what it is intended to do about his affairs, and also what the possible consequences will be. It also implies that the social worker will not use any special skills he may possess to persuade the client against his own judgment to fall in with the plan. This latter point is of particular importance, as social workers are often trained in overcoming resistances of this kind,[9] on the grounds that it is really in the client's best interest to fall in with the arrangements that are being made for him. This was all part of the older view already examined that non-conformity was an aberration anyway, and bringing a person back into the fold, no matter how reluctant he might be at first, could only be, if he but knew it, in his best interest.

At the heart of most of what has been said in this chapter is this issue of who decides when there is a problem to be solved, and if there is, what kind of solution is to be sought. A social work contract enables all sides to decide these matters together. In particular it means that the client's perception of his needs is taken seriously. It must now be clear that this has not always been the case in the past. Often caseworkers would distinguish between the kind of help the client said that he required, the so-called 'presenting problem' and his 'real problem'.[10] The presenting problem might be, say, the unmanageable behaviour of an elderly relative, whom the client therefore wished to have placed in a residential home; the real problem might be an overwhelmed housewife, who needed a larger house where interpersonal friction might be less, and some domestic help to give her more time and energy to devote to the old person concerned. In other words, social caseworkers would often purport to distinguish between the felt 'wants' of clients and their 'needs' — what they should have for their own good, which the social worker through his training and experience was better qualified than they to identify.

The first comment to be made about such a claim is that it is patronising and authoritarian. Surely how people feel about their life situation is what really matters in the end. They must know better than other people where the shoe pinches. And also in a free world they must be allowed to go to the devil in their own way. The second thing to be said about the proposition is that it may nevertheless sometimes be true.

Obvious cases such as those involving very young children, or insane people, deluded or obsessed perhaps, may be left out of account — though not all insane persons entirely lack insight, and we also have an obligation, not often met, to listen to a child's side of things and not merely to post him here and there like a parcel, as happens to suit our views or convenience. But there are other cases also where accepting the client's first statement of his problem may be to his disadvantage.

Freud has shown that the reasons for our behaviour may be repressed by us because they threaten our image of ourselves, or, as we believe, our relationships with other people. Because not to know why we do things would put us in danger of dredging-up the unacceptable repressed reason, we have in self-defence to create a plausible alternative, a rationalisation, to account for it.[11] Where this happens, there is a difference between the presenting rational-isation — the account which the client gives to others, including the social worker, or even to himself — and the real problem, and dealing with the rationalisation would be an irrelevance to the latter. Nor need one always postulate repression. We all sometimes take the

33

short- rather than the long-term view, or the line of least resistance instead of facing up to uncomfortable truths. Lack of knowledge and experience can also play its own important part in making it hard for people to understand the real origin of their privations or unhappiness.

An example of this process at work, in a request for the placement of an old person, has already been given. Another might be a demand by a parent for the return of a child to his home on the grounds that he was unhappy in his residential placement. So he might be, and this might be a justification for his return home; but he might be unhappy because the institution is at last beginning to have some influence on him. Finding the process of changing his behaviour to be difficult, he would prefer to avoid it if he could. These examples are quite apart from any deliberately false explanations, to save face or make for personal gain.

Sometimes the presenting problem seems to be readily understandable in common-sense terms, and the so-called 'real problem' to be more far-fetched. This does not necessarily mean that it does not exist. The unconscious reason is repressed because it is by definition unacceptable — often as much to us as to the client who repressed it in the first place. An example is the bully in a children's home who looks as if he needs discipline and deflation, but is really compensating by his over-bearing behaviour for deep-seated feelings of inadequacy. After all, bullying implies attacking the weak — feeling powerful on the cheap. His presenting behaviour may suggest that he needs 'taking down a peg or two', whereas the reality may well be that he needs 'building-up': that he is down too many 'pegs' already. Similarly with the petty criminal who offers the plausible explanation that he steals because it is easier than working. Plausible that is, until one realises that he spends much time and effort stealing very little, with quite frequent spells in prison in between. His rationalisation may nourish his ego, but it also leads to a purely deterrent approach to his problems which is very wide of the mark. Punishment is not needed to make his crime unprofitable to him; it already is unprofitable enough.

So even if one rejects the view that the dominant culture is always right, with its accompanying 'sickness assumption', it does not follow, either, that the client is always right. How to reconcile such a discovery with the idea of the social work contract is not easy. There is no way in which one can justify the social worker's dictating to clients, but at least he has to be given time to convince them that they have got it wrong. This may not always be a short time. Some emotional defences against painful truths are very powerful indeed, and it will require all the skill which the social worker can summon if they are to be circumvented. But in the end he has to accept the logic of a social worker-client relationship; if he cannot obtain willing acquiescence in the kind of contract he is able to offer, social work is not possible. He also has his rights in the situation, and must be permitted to withdraw if the terms of the contract are unacceptable to him.

Criminals offer a special kind of challenge to the idea of the social work contract. Inadequate petty thieves may not make crime pay, but others do and could therefore be expected often to refuse to co-operate in any measures intended to take this kind of gain away from them. Society will then no doubt justify itself in taking steps to protect itself either by long-term containment, or by rehabilitative efforts involving manipulation of the client's beliefs, rather than working towards agreement on a contract. Matza (though hostile for other reasons to the idea of rehabilitation) would presumably see less difficulty here. If, as he argues, criminals do feel uneasy about their deviation from commonly accepted standards, there is a basis here for arguing with and perhaps eventually convincing them. But failing this, unilateral attempts to bring about change in people, though not social work, are at least selling a popular product — a consensus, accepted according to Matza by everybody but them.

We need Mill to remind us that the majority are not always right. Enforced conformity may be justifiable if it is the act of a legitimately constituted authority acting against a serious threat to the common interest. What is probably never justifiable is the psychological sleight-of-hand by which people may be manipulated into conformity. Let us face up to the element of compulsion involved. We shall then be clear about how big the threat to the general interest needs to be to justify such action.

Chapter four

Selection

Social work, alas, is no universal panacea, and that is particularly true of residential social work. As we have seen, there is reason to believe that placement in a residential establishment sometimes does more harm than good. In what cases then is it desirable? To the social worker, this question will take a personalised form: should this particular client be placed in a residential community, or be helped in some other way?

The answer will depend partly of course on the client and his needs, but not wholly so. In deciding to admit him you are also making a decision about the composition of the inmate population of the institution, and this must inevitably affect how it operates. So one has to have regard for the effect which a particular kind of placement policy will have upon the efficiency of the institution itself. This would have implications extending far beyond the particular client whose placement is under consideration for it may impair (or enhance) the service provided for all its residents.

Let us first consider the kinds of situation in which it seems desirable, in the client's own interest, to provide social work service for him in a residential setting. The most obvious case is that in which, for one reason or another, his home is adjudged unsuitable, unsuitability meaning, in this context, likely to hamper his progress towards the goals set for social work with him.

In the past this has commonly been the justification for placing children, though gradually the criteria for unsuitability have changed. At one time, a dirty and disordered home was all that was required, but gradually emotional factors in the child's home life have begun to be seen as more significant. A squalid home, in itself, would now be treated as important only if it involved a risk to the child's health, or was hampering his progress, for instance in school. It would loom larger in the case of an old or a handicapped person, wanting to make himself comfortable but unable to look after himself properly. Generally speaking, it would depend on how bad the home was, and whether the social worker felt it might be possible to bring about some improvement in it. Inadequacies of diet, health care or safety in the home would, of course, call more imperatively for action.

But otherwise, if the emotional climate of the home was warm and secure, it would usually be felt that the child should stay there. Neighbours and county councillors are usually less tolerant of such conditions, and there is often some pressure on social workers to 'rescue' a child from such a 'bad home', even though the low standards concerned may do little harm except to the aesthetic sense of the complainants. Indeed a home (like a residential institution) can often be too clean: standards can be so high that it is almost impossible for children to be relaxed and natural. Also there are homes where children are provided with every physical amenity, but little or no love. Not that one should fall into the opposite trap: of romanticising the sub-standard home. It often does go with child neglect, and low standards of social training.

So a basic criterion for placement is the apparently irremediable lack of a warm and supportive emotional environment in the home. To this must be added unwillingness or inability on the part of the responsible relatives to co-operate in the social work measures aimed at assisting the client. The use of the word 'irremediable', above, should be noted for future reference.

Although the discussion so far has been concerned solely with children, much the same applies to other kinds of prospective resident. Children need love in order to mature and make a good social adjustment, as well as to make their daily lives happy. Old people have no maturing and adjusting to do, but they do need both affection, and a willingness on the part of others to assist and support them often in spite of their elderly foibles. Such tolerance will not be found where love is lacking. The criteria for the placement of all chronically dependent clients, such as the elderly or the handicapped, are going to be similar, and will also include their inability to find the kindly supervision, and prompt assistance from others, which is necessary if they are to manage their lives outside a residential community. The provisions which can be made for them through the home nursing service, the social workers in the Social Services Department, the home help service, meals on wheels, etc. are invaluable, but provide only discontinuous supervision. They are no substitute for the vigilant relative or neighbour. All of this is on the assumption that they are physically and mentally able to cope anyway.

There is a further demand which is made on their relatives, and also on the relatives of the mentally ill client in the community. They have to be willing to tolerate the public embarrassment which the client may sometimes cause them. A mentally disturbed person may shout or behave in a bizarre way in public. An old man or woman may be incontinent, or find it difficult to eat quietly and cleanly. The physical appearance or gait of a subnormal relative may attract attention in the street. It is only too easy, when something like this happens, either to try to dissociate oneself from the offending person in the eyes of other people, with all the rejection which this implies, or to rush him home and see that he doesn't often go out again to 'show you up like that'.

One may not always be justified in asking relatives to carry such heavy burdens. Times have changed, and it is no longer taken for granted that a daughter, for example, should sacrifice her marriage prospects, or if married her family, in order to care for an ageing father or mother. Similarly child care experts nowadays present parents with a formidable list of demands on behalf of their children, forgetting that the parents themselves also have the right to 'life, liberty and the pursuit of happiness'. There is no suggestion that social workers should attempt to dissuade relatives from immolating themselves, but it does raise questions about how far they should go in trying to persuade them to do so. And in making such a decision, the social worker will have regard to whether the relative faces special difficulties in meeting these obligations — through his own educational or intellectual limitations, existing family obligations, poor housing conditions and so on.

It is now possible to examine the very important implications of the word 'irremediable' used above when describing the unsatisfactory emotional conditions in the home which might give rise to a residential placement. An 'unsatisfactory home' is a negative reason for placement. The person is to be placed not because of any positive values which the residential community possesses, but because the home is not, as it stands, a place in which social work can be carried on. Indeed, in the absence of such positive values, and in view of the danger of institutionalisation, the onus is very much on the social worker to prove to his own satisfaction that removal from home is desirable. This means that if social work in relation to the home environment itself, either prior to or concurrent with the work with the client, was likely to bring about enough improvement, this would be the method of choice. In some cases it might make residential placement unnecessary; in others such placement might need to be only short-term while the home situation was being remedied.

There is one final caveat to all this. In many cases the difficulties which social work seeks to alleviate have not arisen in the client's life in isolation from his social setting. Parents or other relatives may also be implicated in them, and improvement in the client's situation is then not going to be brought about without some change on their part also, even if a decision has been made to place him in residential care.

Once more the classic illustrations are to be found in child care, though the principle involved has wider relevance. A child's difficult behaviour may be best understood as his reaction to the way in which his parents are dealing with him; or even as a result of the feelings of insecurity engendered in him by their failure to get on with each other. Where this is the case, removing the child from home would only put the problem into cold storage. Parent-parent and parent-child relationships can only be realistically improved while the parties are in touch with each other, able to learn out of current experience how to understand and to tolerate one another. This may be more stressful for everybody, including the social worker, than separating them, and may seem to contrast unfavourably with the speedy improvement in the child's behaviour and the parents' attitude to him which often follows removal from home. But the stress is there because the problem is active, and consequently accessible to social work. The success of the alternative of residential placement is then only apparent; the child and his parents are no longer in daily irritating company with each other. And when separated their desire to feel secure and loveworthy often leads them to build up idealised pictures of one another. When the child returns home, the unimproved reality reasserts itself only too soon.

Nothing in what has been said argues finally against placing a client because of the stress caused by his presence at home. We have already seen that this may be necessary on a temporary basis in order to produce a climate in which, when he returns home, social work may be attempted with more success. It may also be justified to relieve the intolerable burdens which his behaviour may impose on his relatives or the public. It is to be hoped that his spell away from home for this reason might need to be only temporary also: that a rest from him might be sufficient, perhaps with the aid of some help or guidance from the social worker. But it is not impossible to think also of long-term placement, but with the welfare of other people in mind for once. The persistent or dangerous criminal is only an extreme example of this kind of case. Whom the social worker in such a situation should consider to be his client; how to balance disservice to one person against a service to another — these are problems in social work ethics, which every social worker has to solve for himself.

In addition to the negative reason, i.e. that a client's home environment is unsuitable, there is the more positive justification for seeking a residential placement for him: that facilities or opportunities are available in the residential setting which could not be provided in any other way. Some of these opportunities could arise out of the residential and group nature of the experience of living in an institution. Others would be less specific to the setting, but consist of the material facilities and amenities which are considered necessary for the clients' progress, and which the home can provide.

In the last chapter we dissected the residential institution in its role as a total institution, and found that as an artificial community it bound residents to it in such a way as to unfit them for life outside. But there are virtues in that very isolation from the outside society, even though if it continues too long it institutionalises those who are subject to it. By means of it residents are sheltered from the *Sturm und Drang* of every day, gaining a tranquillity which can become either a way of life for the long-term resident; or for others a basis for reconsideration, and ultimately for a further assault on existence outside.

Institutions will differ in the permeability of their boundaries, and therefore the degree of protection which they provide. They may even vary in this respect at different times, or in respect of different clients. But to an extent which will depend on the degree of insularity attained, the society of the institution can diverge from that outside, opening up the possibility of actually shaping it to achieve particular social work purposes. Thus it is possible to plan all or any aspects of the experience of inmates on a twenty-four-hours-a-day, seven-days-a-week basis; utilise the ready-made peer group of the home, with all the possibilities for personal influence this offers; and benefit from the fact that an institutional population does not have to be motivated to attend treatment sessions, but is available all the time. The fact that one can actually exploit such features of residential life, to the point if desired at which the institution becomes a therapeutic community, is offered as an important objection (with others) to the complete replacement of the mental hospital by care for mental patients out in the community. These are aspects of regime development to which close attention will have to be given at a later stage. For the present it is enough to note that the shelter which an institution can provide, and the availability of a special kind of regime may represent positive reasons for deciding to essay social work with certain kinds of individual in a residential rather than a home setting.

We have examined two criteria for selection in which the interests of the particular aspirant are paramount: (a) where his home is unsuitable, (b) where the residential community offers scope for helping him which would not otherwise be available. We must now consider what effect his admission is likely to have on the effectiveness of the work of the institution as a whole. What seems at first sight to be a fairly straightforward consideration here is whether he would require special attention or the use of special facilities, thus overburdening the home or limiting what could be done for the other residents. Particularly severe physical or mental handicap might have this result; but so equally might unmanageable or disordered behaviour, say, by a very difficult child, a psychopathic offender, or an old person with a propensity for wandering off. Such clients might need residential care even more than others, so that the question becomes one, not so much of whether they should be placed but where.

However, these problems can also be seen in a more constructive light. Meeting special needs of the sort referred to may be seen as absorbing staff time, or on the other hand as providing an opportunity for 'helping' by other inmates, which can be as valuable for them as for those receiving the help. There are a variety of possibilities, ranging from a 'special friend', who comes to be called on whenever his friend is in difficulties, to the acceptance of a communal responsibility for somebody, which gives a sense of purpose to the whole inmate group. An example of the latter concerned an epileptic child in a residential school for maladjusted children. In spite of medication his fits continued to occur, and in a very unpredictable fashion, but this did not limit his activities as much as it might have done because the other children understood his condition, and were able to look after him and make him comfortable, wherever and whenever a seizure began. Instead of being a burden on the institution, he became an asset to it: a focus around and from which co-operative action grew, as well as an opportunity for 'naughty' children who had so often been made to feel guilty and unloveworthy, to feel that they were doing something good for a change. The freedom of movement and sense of being cherished which it gave to the epileptic himself was a further gain.

This example calls attention to the composition of the institutional group as a factor, in any discussion of selection policy. It is a very fundamental factor. The residential community is really a residential group, and the residential experience a by-product of the group relationships established in the institution. Those relationships and that experience cannot help but be shaped at least in part by the kind of people who constitute the group. Cattell has shown experimentally that the general character of a group is strongly influenced by the characteristics of its members.[1] It is obviously impossible to aim at producing a particular kind of institution without having at least some regard to the kinds of people who live in it and therefore create its character. This of course has been long acknowledged in the rule-of-thumb practice of institutions even though its implications have not been fully appreciated by them. Usually they have confined themselves to removing 'difficult' residents, significantly enough describing the latter as 'people who don't fit in', but without going further and making explicit the fact that it is to a particular regime that they are failing to adjust.

The extent to which an institution can select its inmate population varies. Some homes run by voluntary organisations can pick and choose freely, and this enables them sometimes to develop a very specialised character. They may also select on a less defensible basis, e.g. according to a person's religion or whether he can pay the fees. Publicly run institutions often have to take whoever comes along, especially if the inmates in question are being committed under some kind of legal restraint, e.g. prisoners, or patients received into a mental hospital under a compulsory order. It is therefore a counsel of perfection to suggest that all institutions should choose their residents strictly according to the requirements of the group situation. Nevertheless even within the public sector there may be scope for allocation between different institutions with those requirements in mind. And if this is not possible the smaller groups into which all residential institutions of any size are divided can provide a basis for purposive grouping.

There are two main ways in which the composition of a group operates to determine its character, and therefore the nature of the institutional regime to which it contributes. One is through the interactions which take place between individual group members, and the other, through its share in forming the climate of the group-as-a-whole. Though logically separable, these are, in practice, closely related.

A particular pattern of individual interaction is an obvious consequence of constituting a group in a particular way. Certain kinds of people will antagonise each other, or provide some other kind of mutual stimulation. For example a number of domineering individuals may contend for leadership in the group, or a number of exhibitionistic members for its attention. There will often also be more specific causes of friction. For reasons which no doubt their backgrounds could explain, some people may find certain personality traits in other people irritating. Hence the anti-authority member who cannot bear what he might call the 'creepers' in the group, or the defensively masculine individual who is disturbed and angered by what he sees as feminine traits in other male members of the group. Sociometric studies of children in institutions show that different homes can vary widely in the extent to which they generate accepting or rejecting attitudes among residents.[2] In the light of the importance of group composition to overall group climate some part of this difference must be due to individual clashes of personality.

Some individual interactions on the other hand will be supportive and co-operative. Usually they will be congenial and possibly advantageous to all parties concerned, sometimes satisfying complementary needs in almost a symbiotic fashion. Thus a timid person may link up with somebody who has strong protective tendencies; or an explosive individual welcome the restraining influence of a member disturbed by his outburst, who makes it his job to try to calm him down. Some people cannot tolerate any overt expressions of hostility and spend much of their time in conciliatory activity of one sort or another. This may sometimes merely make it more difficult for the group to face up to its and its members' inter-personal problems, but it may also serve a more constructive purpose in maintaining the unity of the group at a time of very great tension.

There may some time be a more ominous side even to the dove-tailing of needs, as when one resident with a need to dominate finds somebody among his fellows who actually enjoys being bullied — perhaps even physically. For two such individuals to pair up will merely serve to reinforce possibly undesirable traits in both. The follower (or crafty instigator) who eggs-on or manipulates an unperceptive fellow-resident who has a need for flattery and a sense of importance, into anti-social behaviour could be participating in a similarly unhelpful coalescence of needs. The list will be a long one, but the principle is clear enough. Many would question nowadays if it really mattered if two inmates with homosexual inclinations met up with each other in the institution, but most managements, with general public attitudes to the institution on their minds, would be concerned about it.

It would be the aim of a rational selection or allocation policy to construct groups which would maximise desirable interactions, and minimise the more damaging ones. The latter aim does not always necessitate the exclusion of problem inmates. It may sometimes be enough to add some neutralising element to the mix: a peacemaker, a competitor, a debunker, etc.

Nobody who has worked with groups — in an institution, the classroom, or even a committee — will be satisfied with a description of group-life in terms solely of individual interactions. Gradually as members get to know each other better, a group tends to become more unified. Members begin to think more in terms of 'we' than of 'I', and to become sensitive to what other members think of them. As a result of these developments, individual members accommodate their ideas and behaviour to those of others, and group norms about 'right and proper' behaviour begin to emerge. This is a matter of simple observation, but it has also been demonstrated experimentally in the psychological laboratory, e.g.

by Sherif and Asch.[3] Schachter[4] also showed how a group focused all its activity on any members who expressed non-conformist views — until they capitulated, when interest in them disappeared.

The development of group norms in this way is clearly going to affect the individual interactions referred to above. The more idiosyncratic ideas are going to be either suppressed completely or driven underground: Asch's research showed that one solution found by his 'deviants' in trying to turn the wrath of the group was apparently to accept the group's judgments while secretly holding to their own beliefs. Other views not so irreconcilable with those of the group, would tend to change in the direction of conformity, becoming, as it were, 'variations on a theme'.

This formidable pressure towards conformity could be either helpful or otherwise to the aims of social work in a residential community. It could for instance foster co-operation with the staff and an optimistic spirit among residents, or antagonism and depression.[5] The important point is that the selection of residents must be carried out with such effects in mind. This is not to suggest that the character of the group-as-a-whole is entirely determined by its composition. Like individual character, it is shaped partly by its life-experience, including its interaction with its environment. In the case of an institutional group, that environment includes not only its physical environment, such as its site and buildings, and the satisfactions and privations of institutional life, but also the interpersonal and intergroup environment, notably relationships with the staff and with people from outside the institution, such as relatives, visiting tradesmen, the neighbouring community, but above all, the staff. The influence of the staff must be emphasised because they are there to try to achieve the social work aims of the institution, and therefore have a responsibility for trying to produce a group climate which is favourable to that purpose.

Environmental influences like these notwithstanding, group composition remains an essential element. Cattell's research, already cited, puts that beyond dispute. The character of a newly formed group emerges out of a process of mutual accommodation between those group members, who are also presented with a demand for adjustment from their environment. This three-sided interaction is complex, but much of the bargaining which takes place with the 'outside', is by the group as an entity, i.e. after it has achieved some degree of solidarity. Indeed, that very solidarity is often strengthened by members making favourable comparisons between the group and other groups or even by uniting in a common hostility to outsiders. The exception is the staff, whose responsibility for what goes on in the group requires them to be constantly active in it.

A group, however composed, passes through a phase of individual insecurity and mistrust, to a stage at which at least enough confidence has been generated to make it possible to express open rivalry or hostility. Links, usually between pairs, and of either a negative or positive kind follow, as oases of support in what otherwise appears to members at this time to be a rather arid and threatening world. Gradually compromises are reached, leadership struggles resolved, and individuals begin to accept the roles that the group has assigned to them. It is in clarifying some of these interpersonal situations that environmental pressures sometimes achieve a degree of direct influence. Thus if the internal struggle becomes inconvenient the staff may intervene, or the contending individuals may lay claim to or enlist the aid of outsiders. Thus an aspiring leader may say of his rival, 'If he has his way instead of me, there's going to be trouble and the authorities will have to interfere. Nobody will like that.'

The acceptance by a member of a group role relates not only to toeing the group line as far as behaviour is concerned, but actually becoming the group's representative or spokesman in certain situations or aspects of group life. Thus certain persons always lead in any hostility towards the staff, while others are relied on by the group to 'pour oil on troubled waters' and so on. It is of the utmost importance to recognise the group character of such behaviour: the individual is not speaking or acting solely for himself, but for the group. Therefore if, for example, one wishes to change his behaviour it is usually necessary to change the conditions within the group which make it want somebody to act in this way for it. As an example one could take the case of the subversive or defiant resident. All the staff pray for the day when he leaves, believing that this will solve all their problems. Eventually the old person in question dies, the difficult child leaves. Almost at once somebody else, whose behaviour till then has been exemplary, steps into his shoes, for as it appears, the group need expressed in this behaviour remains unsatisfied. Of course not all individual behaviour in a matured group is representative of the group-as-a-whole in this way, and one of the skills which the residential social worker needs to acquire is to recognise when it is, and when it is purely the expression of an individual motivation.

The staff will have been active throughout, first of course in monitoring the composition of the group, but then in guiding its development towards a group character which will be favourable to the attainment of the desired objective. They will want to produce a cohesive group in which the group opinion counts for something, on the assumption that what the group will be transmitting are desirable norms, or a desirable frame of mind. They will want also to deal effectively with group trends which are going to hamper the achievement of the social work task, and particularly with those which threaten the unity of the group. Such trends otherwise can lead not only to an impotent group, but also a group which will lose its members — probably corporeally but at least in spirit.

Yet unity is not everything, at any rate in institutions concerned with change, i.e. those of a nurtural or rehabilitative character. In the interests of unity (and their own comfort) staff are perhaps sometimes too inclined to exclude the 'trouble-maker', forgetting that both in terms of his impact in individual interaction, and in the education of the group, he more than pays his way. The group itself also feels threatened by him, and will collude with the staff in attempting to either assimilate him or drive him out. The peace of mind of the staff (or of the group) is not the purpose of the operation; constructive elements of conflict disturb complacency, cause people to try to understand themselves and each other, and in these and other ways provide the group with a mainspring, a motivation, which keeps it alive and active. The alternative would be an inert mechanism: a mutual admiration society, in which little or nothing happens.

The case may be different where peace and quiet is the aim, mainly institutions with an asylum function, like homes for the elderly or the chronically handicapped. Change in behaviour is not a prime objective; their residents' long-term comfort is the end towards which selection policy mainly needs to be directed. But even here, too uneventful a life may simply encourage the ever-present danger of a decline into apathy. The difficult old lady may come to represent a valuable focus for interest, discussion and even malice — and possibly enjoy it. The suggestion occasionally made that children and old people often get on very well together, and therefore might be looked after in the same home, has also this value of helping to keep alive the social interest of the elderly, though there would have to be ways also in which the two groups could be protected from each other at certain times of the day.

At first sight it might almost look as if the membership of an institutional group could be so composed that the social work task proceeded without any help from outside. The individual interactions would provide the necessary enlightening learning experiences while background morale and an appropriate degree of social integration would be brought about by the influence of the group climate. This is no more than a theoretical possibility. As we have seen, administrative, legal, or moral considerations prevent people from being included or excluded purely on grounds of their utility to the group. But there is also a more practical objection. People's needs just are not complementary enough for such a policy to be workable. You admit Mr A for a particular contribution that he can make to the group, and Mr B for another, only to find that they have an undesirable effect on each other.

This is where the social worker comes in. He expects a fairly stable contribution from group members, on the basis of which alone he can predict their effect on the group. He, on the other hand, must be flexible, prepared to make up his own activity for any and every shortcoming which the imperfect composition of the group produces in its effects on its members. Knowing his own limitations, he will therefore constitute a group in such a way that he feels he can achieve this: in everyday language, he constructs a group which he feels he can handle. Thus not all 'ideal' groups will be the same; much will depend on the qualities of the social workers involved. This presentation of the social worker as the joker in the pack is intended not merely as a contribution to selection policy, but also represents a basic formulation of the role of the social worker in a residential (or any other kind of) group which will require further development in due course.

Any discussion of selection will be incomplete if it does not give some consideration to the point of view of the person selected. Two factors will be crucial here: how desperate he feels his situation outside to have become, and the image he has of what going into a home means. The more apprehensive an old person is about his safety, or about managing his life outside, the more he will come to see admission to the home as a desirable solution. But only if expectations from it match up to his needs.

His prior image of residential care may have been built up by information from a number of sources, not all of which will possess a very accurate picture of residential life themselves. For instance there is still resistance among older people to going into an old people's home or a mental hospital, on the grounds that if you do, it means that your life is finished. Because the staff also recognise that, nobody will try very hard to keep you alive, and you will die soon after admission. Juvenile offenders committed to a community home often have an exaggeratedly punitive idea of what it will be like. Knowing somebody else who has entered a particular home is usually the best way to dissipate such fears. Sometimes as in the case of a formerly respectable citizen, who is making his first contact with a prison when he serves his sentence in one, the reality may prove to be much worse than the expectation. It is often a shock, for instance, to discover how much at the mercy of other prisoners you are: how little protection from them the staff can give you.

After admission, the new resident will be able to correct his pre-judgments in the light of experience, but old people particularly may be slow to revise their view of the home even when it runs directly counter to what they see happening around them. Prejudices die hard in the elderly. And whatever your age, it is not too difficult to reinterpret what is happening to you in a way which does not controvert your established beliefs. Thus a refusal by the staff, for good reasons, to agree to a request by a new inmate, easily becomes spite or meanness.

Quite apart from the new resident's reaction to entry into the home as such, he has to adjust himself to norms of behaviour in the institution which may be quite different from those he has always accepted for himself in the past. At the very least, he will find himself having to tolerate a give-and-take with others and perhaps a degree of regulation of his behaviour to which he is unaccustomed, but there may be more than this. Traditional working-class inmates do not conform very easily to the middle-class practices maintained in some residential homes. In the smaller homes it is more likely that senior staff and therefore the regime will have an indigenous working-class flavour, more congenial to the residents for whom the home caters.

An important element in the situation confronting the new inmate is the attitude of the inmate group already in possession. They will add their own quota to the demands which the institution makes on him, and may be quick to condemn him if he puts a foot wrong — like talking too much 'before he has been in the home five minutes', or sitting in a chair to which long custom has given another inmate a prescriptive right. He finds himself, in fact, facing the group-as-a-whole, with its established code of behaviour, and assigned roles, and also with the difficulty it has in finding a place for someone else within the tight network of safe mutual relationships it has been able to establish between its various members.

The task of the social worker is to ease this transition for his new client. He has to help him to see the institution as it really is, dispelling his prejudices; and also supporting him in his efforts to do what is required of him. Suspicion and failures can be expected, calling for a good deal of tolerance and patience. In accordance with his function as the flexible element in the residential group the staff member will also have to work towards making the existing inmate group more welcoming towards the newcomer. This means recognising the problems it has in doing this, and helping it to solve those problems. His presence during early confrontations between the two sides will enable him to reassure the group about the new member, and buoy up the latter's determination to secure acceptance for himself.

What is known about 'pairing' in groups points to an important practical step which can be taken. If a link can be found for him with somebody who is already well accepted in the group the battle is virtually won. The basis for such a partnership could be having worked in the same job or come from the same area, having a common interest, or a symbiotic bond of the sort discussed earlier in this chapter — or even just personal liking. A danger to be avoided is of his linking himself with another outcast. Of course people who come into residence at the same time are often thrown together by their common need, and such a relationship may be a great support to both of them during their period in limbo.

These early days are bound to be stressful. A co-operative and friendly group character in a home, with no need therefore for the group to find scapegoats whether among newcomers, or anywhere else, will make it easier. For the rest, the responsibility is on the shoulders of the social worker. He has to strive for assimilation, and meanwhile through his own demeanour and what tolerance he can exact from established residents, to make the home seem, to his incoming client, an acceptable alternative to the life he has left behind.

Chapter five

Order

The demand for order in the institution is to a large extent a response to the public insistence on effective containment. In their repository role, institutions are primarily concerned with ensuring that no echoes of the problems within them escape to trouble the rest of us. So behavioural conformity has to be insisted on. As we have seen in talking about penal institutions, there are limits in practice in the extent to which this can be achieved, and staff often content themselves instead with conformity on the surface. This is in spite of the fact that they may be aware of an anti-conformist inmate society underneath.

But containment is not limited to the enforcement of behavioural orderliness. Unacceptable social behaviour is so associated in our society with personal uncleanliness and domestic squalor, that acquiescence in these respects also becomes necessary to reassure respectable society that its problem citizens are being made to toe the line. There are, of course, good reasons for the maintenance of hygienic conditions in an institution, and no doubt these play their part in influencing public attitudes, and through them the attitudes of the staff. But they are also often presented as the reason, when they are no more than rationalisations for underlying containment objectives. The part played by 'show' in the standards of physical care in a home are revealing. There was for example the footbath, of which the head of a boys' home was inordinately proud, but which was hardly ever used because it might become soiled and worn. There is also the familiar special clean-up, or special menu, because the committee are due to pay a visit. The parallel between such practices and the willingness to accept superficial behavioural conformity in exchange for the real thing is close.

Elsewhere in this book, such tendencies have been called a custodial compromise, and they do indeed represent a kind of implicit compact between staff and inmates, made necessary by the impossibility of their surviving together in the institution without some give-and-take. But there is the third party to these trans-actions, the public at large, and some part of what goes on is to satisfy them. Not that the public is entirely deceived. No real change in personal commitment by inmates is necessary to meet the require-ments of respectable society it seems, but only enough lip-service to ensure that problems are effectively buried within the home.

It is intended in the present chapter to discuss physical care and social order in the institution, both in this apparently socially functional sense, and in relation to the more defensible social work purposes which they can serve.

It has already been argued that personal or domestic squalor, though always a concern of social work, is not by itself necessarily seen as justifying residential placement. Where it does play a part, it will usually be because of its effect on the health or development of the individual, or when (as for example with old people) the provision of a comfortable and healthy home environment is itself the main aim of social work. It will then be the task of the institution to supply those physical amenities which the client lacked in his own home.

This does not mean that actually carrying out the duties required to supply these physical needs is necessarily a part of social work. Some would argue that it is. Especially with young children, mentally handicapped persons, and withdrawn mental patients, a caring attitude can be communicated through physical care — touching, feeding, cleaning, setting to sleep — where words might mean very little. Many nurses also take this view, accounting for the fact that they still value the time they spend in activities which are more domestic than medical in character. Against this is the view that mothering activities of this kind are best performed in a natural and instinctual rather than a professional fashion. For their own sake, as it were, rather than with some ulterior motive in mind. They are also very time-consuming; the mainstream social work activities in themselves probably need all the time that can be found for them.

There can be no doubt, however, that it is the responsibility of the social worker, at least to see that an appropriate standard of provision is maintained, and this raises the delicate question, to which attention will be given later, of the relationships between social workers and other staff in a home. It also raises another issue which must be dealt with now, as to what is an appropriate standard of provision.

There can be no argument but that the physical environment must be healthy. So the diet must be balanced and sufficient, and to ensure that it is eaten, it must be attractive and varied. Standards of hygiene and health care must be adequate. But given all this, and also the limited degree of neatness which is required for an institution to run at all, how much further should one go? We are back here of course with the argument already mentioned about whether a place might not be too neat to be comfortable to live in. Some would argue that such standards should be purely functional: to enable residents to live comfortably and healthily together. Beyond this, you are either catering to the narcissistic housewifely instincts of the domestic staff, or to some public conception that an institution ought to gleam with cleanliness. Few committee members who run their fingers along ledges in search of dust during their weekly visit to the institution would expect such unnatural standards in their own homes. None of which would matter if it was not, as it so often is, at the expense of residents, who are required not to use the spotless front staircase, expected to change their shoes whenever they come indoors, not to pull the chairs higgledy-piggledy about the room, ruffling the carpet in the process, not to leave their things about, and so on. One staff member in a children's home was once heard to say, 'This would be a fine place to be in if there were no children here.' Having failed to get rid of the children (or other residents) some institutions seem to want to remove every other sign of their existence except their unfortunately unavoidable physical presence. There is also the therapeutic case sometimes argued in respect of psychiatric institutions or institutions for difficult children, that standards need to be relaxed even further in order to reduce the pressure on inmates whose tolerance of frustration is very low.

Against these views are those who argue that a ship-shape institution makes for a ship-shape mind; the standards enforced by the institution become habitual and automatic, so that by living in an institution which is clean and tidy, residents themselves become clean and tidy. Where they were previously living in bad conditions, it is suggested, more than normally rigorous demands have to be made on them, for there are bad previous habits to be broken — an interesting inversion of the idea of 'positive discrimination' as formerly understood. This appears sometimes in almost a deterrent guise: they have been dirty in the past and must be taught that this kind of thing is not allowed in XYZ Home. The respectable public's attitude of 'They're lucky to be there; they should show their appreciation of that fact by doing better than everybody else' goes even further in being actually retributive. Residents it seems have a debt to pay off to society in exchange for being allowed to live in the institution.

A desire to present a favourable image to the committee and the general public always plays a part in the minds of institution staff. This is understandable. We all have to make our way in life, and so long as committee members and ratepayers look on institutions as in debt to society, or as civic status symbols, staff will feel under pressure to present to the world the right kind of well-scrubbed appearance. And there is a less selfish aspect: if you can make a good impression on the committee or the public you are more likely to get resources and other forms of support from them. This accounts for and may to some extent justify the 'open-day' clean-up which inmates and even insightful commentators like Goffman often criticise. If you feel that the public demand for neatness is not in the interest of residents, but that failing to satisfy it will harm that interest in other ways, what have you left but subterfuge?

What has been said so far has focused on the coercive aspect of physical care. Just as important is its supportive side. Old folks who have been unable to feed themselves properly are now, in the home, getting good meals and can even have a paper to read or a radio or television set to listen to. Children are no longer running about in shoes that let in the water, or chilled to the bone in thin clothes: and because they can now have football boots or dancing shoes like everybody else, can at last hold their heads erect in school. For the adult whose previous household chaos could only have deepened his sense of hopelessness and despair, a new life of system and cleanliness can almost magically simplify all sorts of things for him. Special architectural features like ramps for a wheel-chair, and appliances and aids will help the staff as much as they do the residents.

There will always of course be disagreement about standards of physical care. The level to be aimed at ought to depend on circumstances, especially on the needs of the particular group of residents, but as we do not always know enough to be sure how those needs can best be satisfied, disagreements will continue. And some of the divergences between institutions will be caused by differences in the values, prejudices, backgrounds, and ambitions of the staff concerned. It is a part of the role of the social worker to recognise the influence which motivations like these are having on life in the institution, and to ensure that it is kept in its place.

The standards of physical care in an institution and the methods used in maintaining them do, as we have seen, often reflect more general attitudes of the staff towards such questions as what institutions are for, and how inmates ought to be treated. Thus it will often be found that the institutions which are most spick and span often achieve these conditions by means of a discipline which also animates other aspects of the regime. Such establishments are often rather impersonal, and lay emphasis on obedience, and on *what* people do rather than *why* they do it. There is thus a link between physical care and the kind of personal relationships which exist between staff and residents; the importance of personal relationships will be explored in the next chapter. The link with the control of behaviour in the institution is seen to be no less close. It is such parallels between various aspects of life in an institution, emerging out of the social philosophy and personal motivations of those responsible for setting its tone, which gives a regime as such its unity, and recognisable character.

It is the debate about behavioural control in the institution which now calls for attention. On the one hand there are those who argue that discipline and obedience are good in themselves: sound virtues in any society. There are also sometimes echoes of nineteenth-century 'less eligibility': an implication that people in institutions ought not really to be there and so should be deterred by a rigorous discipline. Such a deterrent attitude is, of course, strongest in penal institutions, but not entirely lacking in other settings. Finally it is argued that social order in the institution is necessary in order that it may operate efficiently. The further contention that a firm control over inmate behaviour also establishes desirable habits, and therefore brings about general changes for the better in inmate social adjustment will be considered when Change is under discussion in Chapter 7.

The first two arguments are too inconsistent with present-day social morality to call for much in the way of refutation. It is difficult to make a case for unthinking obedience, in a society which espouses the values of self-determination and democracy. Social agencies which operate on principles which are so incongruous with the general culture are soon under pressure to change. We see this even in situations where there might be a practical case for them. The case for normal trade unionism among the police, including the right to strike, is constantly being canvassed by the Police Federation, which is the nearest thing to a union which the police are allowed at present. Prison staffs already possess (and exercise) these rights. Although the special role of the police and prison officers might make unionism look to some like a very dangerous innovation indeed, the right for workers to organise in order to protect their rights is widely accepted and makes occupations in which it is not conceded look anomalous and unfair. Even prisoners have from time to time demanded the right to have a trade union, and their organisation PROP (Preservation of the Rights of Prisoners), though unrecognised by the Home Office, was at one time able to bring about strikes, occupations of the roof, etc. at a number of British prisons.

So it is with inmate control for its own sake. There may still be people who deep down would feel happier in a more authoritarian society, but are also children of the late twentieth century, incurably infected by its values. Given the power to establish their own system of government in an institution, they tend towards discipline and control, but cannot help but be ambivalent about it, and therefore vulnerable to pressures from outside. They find themselves forced to justify an undemocratic regime by arguments about democracy: largely that the self-discipline required for self-government can be attained by the misfits with whom they deal only as a result of a prior experience of being disciplined by other people. The effect of such externally imposed control in a prison in producing the dependent 'old lag' gives the lie to this argument.

There are similar problems facing the less-eligibility[1] argument. Although containment is still the main underlying motive for the use of residential establishments, we pay lip-service to their welfare function, and the present trend towards community care suggests that the former is losing ground to the latter. Although the belief that inmates of institutions are to blame for being there is dying only a slow death, it is surely doomed. There is more validity in the argument that order is required in order for the institution to achieve its aims, though the degree of discipline and obedience exacted may well achieve only formal compliance, which may not be so very helpful.

Some researchers see attitudes of this kind as arising out of personal needs in the minds of people who often run such homes. Psychoanalysts theorise that individuals with an insecure control over their own more turbulent impulses not only have to impose rigid controls over themselves in order to feel safe from those feelings, but must also control those around them.[2] Otherwise the less inhibited behaviour of the people with whom they are in contact might represent too much of a challenge to their own mode of adjustment, and therefore too much of a temptation to their precarious inner balance. This is similar to the more extreme syndrome of the 'authoritarian personality'[3] in which one solves the problem of restraining one's less acceptable tendencies by projecting them on to other people, and thus justifying both the control and punishment of these scapegoat persons. The authoritarian is just as submissive to authority as he is domineering towards anybody under his control. This is because he abdicates his own inner controlling function to anybody in authority over him. The authoritarian syndrome is centred on this tendency to disclaim responsibility, both for one's own impulses and for one's own self-control. The question remains as to why insecure, or authoritarian, individuals should gravitate towards residential care.

Though fewer than in the past, there is little doubt that some have. It can be due only to the attractiveness to them of the traditional total institution, operating on a policy of containment. That the public expect an administrator to run an effective container, supplies him with both a personal crutch and the sense that his values are approved of and thus legitimated by the general public. The kind of regime which emerges allows him to, indeed necessitates, that he control inmates in a way which he finds personally satisfying. There is no suggestion of course that those who oppose strong discipline are less personally motivated.

They tend however to be a more varied group, ranging from belief, on therapeutic grounds, in a highly permissive regime, such as that expounded in the writings of A. S. Neill;[4] or approaches containing elements of self-government, as in the work of Maxwell Jones[5] or David Wills;[6] to more middle-of-the-road methods. The latter often rely on a kind of parental control, in which personal influence is combined with attempts to understand inmates, and while explanations are given for decisions the ultimate power to make them is clearly concentrated in the staff and firmly exercised by them.[7] There is a good deal of overlap: A. S. Neill also used personal influence and self-governing methods, and David Wills, while rejecting a laissez-faire approach to the children in his care, laid great stress on personal relationships.

Starting at the more permissive end, one can discern here a number of possible personal motivations. The more permissive have to be persons who are not panicked or confused by noise and disorder around them. They need to be able to cope with situations on a personal basis as they arise, but nevertheless to keep long-term objectives in mind. In other words a purely tactical ability to meet problems of order on an *ad hoc* basis as they arise is not enough if it means sacrificing the overall aims which the institution has set for itself. Thus it is easy to capitalise on the unpopularity of an interfering old lady in a home in order to shut her up, but by itself it does nothing to realise the asylum aim of making her happy and comfortable within the home.

The regime with less formal discipline is thus no haven for the person with the purely negative qualification of being unable to keep order. Often someone who lacks skill and confidence in doing this sees his salvation in an institution in which (as he believes) order does not have to be maintained, only to discover that he is thrown back on those personal resources in which he feels most deficient. At least the formally structured establishment provided a tradition of order on which he could lean, if only for a time. The analogy is with the stage performer who enters the theatre with a good deal of unearned goodwill from the audience; they have come to enjoy themselves and will put up with much rather than disappoint that expectation. But there is a limit. In the same way residents may come to realise that the discipline which they have taken for granted for so long does indeed have a chink in it.

Because of the primacy given to containment in the traditional institution, staff have tended to be valued mainly for their ability to maintain order. Indeed the staff member with difficulties in this direction is usually stigmatised as 'weak', as though he were suffering from some defect of character, whereas it may often be quite the reverse. It is the sensitive person who really wants to get close to clients, and has enough imagination to envisage failure in controlling them, who often loses confidence within a structure which values discipline more than relationships. He often has much to give if the institution is willing to help him over his difficulty in maintaining order — or wants his contribution enough even to tolerate his other shortcomings.

Another traditional myth is that the ability to maintain order is an inherent personal quality which requires, and indeed is open to no more detailed analysis than that you either have it or you don't. In fact the preservation or failure of order in an institution is a manifestation of personal needs and group processes which is perfectly capable of being understood, and of forming the basis for a programme of staff training. Those who achieve control by the light of nature, do it only by a blinder, more instinctive grasp of the same situations.

Certain guiding principles can be laid down. An individual's acts of opposition may be genuinely personal to the rebel himself, or he may be representing through his behaviour more widespread dissatisfactions within the group. Even where they start as personal they may gain a broader significance if the staff member, in handling them, evokes motives which a number of members share. Thus the staff member's reaction may cause the inmate group to come to see him as unfair, as hostile to traits of the protester which they feel they possess also, as starting out on a campaign which could threaten individual satisfactions or group solidarity, and so on.

But how does the behaviour of an individual resident come to have such group-wide importance? Largely because of the psychological mechanism of identification.[8] Other members inhibited by long-standing habit or by what they see as the threat from the custodians of order, do not need to take the risk of protesting for themselves. They can identify with him as he does so, thus gaining vicarious satisfaction for their needs. But of course this is possible only so long as someone is willing to serve as front-man in this way, so there is pressure in the group for someone to step forward. It is the personal characteristics of such a someone which makes him vulnerable to pressure of this kind. Perhaps his underlying inferiority feelings cause him to need to stand out from the rest, or to win their implicit approval by 'speaking' out for them. Or perhaps his dissatisfactions demand expression more urgently than those of the rest. Or perhaps he is in a general way more anti-authority or more impulsive than they are. That he does speak for more than himself however is shown by the fact that if he is removed from the scene, some other, previously more amenable resident steps into his oppositional role. This will have been a familiar cycle of events to many experienced residential workers. Its bearing on the practical task is surely clear: do not expect to deal with group unrest of this kind merely by concentrating on the person who expresses it for the group.

Sometimes individual acts of defiance escalate into a collective explosion. Such widespread disorder is seen as a major failure by the staff member directly involved, though in the light of the analysis above it was always on the cards as a result of more general features of the regime. One circumstance in which it may occur is if there is a widespread cause of unrest, but the vicarious outlet is blocked, because possible acters-out have been coerced or persuaded into silence. Even then some staff may have a sufficiently formidable image with the group to be able to keep the cork in the bottle for a time.

At other times however the very expression of dissatisfaction by an individual, instead of lowering the tension, detonates the explosion. Redl et al.[9] have spoken of the significance of someone 'doing it first' and by thus assuming most of the responsibility, releasing other more timid souls to follow suit. Presumably this solution, rather than that of vicarious participation, becomes necessary because of the strength of group dissatisfaction. To avoid it calls for early diagnosis of such needs, and action to deal with them. Alternatively, it may result from the perception by the group of a lack of skill or confidence in those in control. As they lose some of their intimidatory authority, inhibitions on direct action are reduced.

Identifying and supplying the group's frustrated needs remains central. They may be a result of failures by the institution (e.g. poor food, a depriving social environment) or of action by the staff member concerned (e.g. unfair punishments), or simply arise out of interactions or developmental needs within the group itself. For instance, members feel unsafe with each other until the group's solidarity is established; they know then that the code of the group will protect them. In the meantime however they have a need, in a world of competing, suspicious and often hostile fellow-residents, to feel safer than they do. In such a situation members will often split off the negative side of their relationships with one another and direct all this suspicion, hostility, etc. on to an outsider, leaving only positive feelings within the group. The group is united in a common rejection of the chosen scapegoat. Sometimes the scapegoat is another group member, sometimes another group — but sometimes it is the houseparent or teacher or other person in charge of the group. It is a painful predicament to be in, but if the staff member can endure it without being thrown off course, it will be temporary. And it can be shortened if he increases the number of opportunities for the group members to interact with one another and so bring their group life to a higher level of maturity.

External coercion is clearly not the only or even perhaps the most effective way of maintaining order; understanding of the group situation can lead to action which does not merely cover-over chronic problems within the institution. Even the grip exercised over inmates by the so-called 'strong disciplinarian' can be analysed, understood, and perhaps be acquired by training. The fear on which it is based probably derives more from inmates' fantasies about their parents than from any punitive reality in the present.[10]

People will also sometimes behave well because they want to please others. There would almost certainly be a period of disorder until residents began to know and like the person in charge of them. And this would be more extensive and last longer if residents' previous experience of discipline had been of the more coercive kind; they need time to test out and understand this new situation.

The adoption of such a policy calls for determination and tolerance on the part of the staff, and will obviously be possible only if it does not run counter to wider policies of the institution, or of its sponsoring agency. In other words, the latter also have to be willing to tolerate the interim period of disorder. It is also going to be a more practicable approach in a home in which small groups are the rule. This does not necessarily mean that large institutions cannot adopt it, but that if they do, they must be run in a small-group fashion, in which particular staff members are assigned to the same small group of residents, and so can build up a relationship with them based on mutual trust and understanding. The consequences of a breakdown of order in such a small group are also going to be much less damaging to the institution and its regime.

Whatever its institutional setting, however, this approach has definite advantages over coercive methods. It leads to less tension between governor and governed: the latter are not held in reluctant subjection by external constraint, but accept their role willingly. Not only does this lay the spectre of indiscipline which seems to haunt those working in institutions, but it drains all the meaning from the word 'discipline' — in the sense of forms of obedience to be maintained at all costs 'in case worse befall'. You can now take 'lip' from an inmate without the fear that as a result the whole institution will fall apart. And the new relationship between staff and residents engenders a more positive attitude towards authority outside as well as within the institution, and also lays a better foundation for the kind of helping relationships required in social work.

Another motive for co-operation between inmates and staff in keeping the institution on an even keel is the value which an orderly institution has for everybody. And in the end this is probably also the main justification for trying to achieve it. A disorderly institution is an uncomfortable one in which to live or work. Interruptions do not occur only when you would like them to; your recreation, your sleep, and your digestion are sometimes going to be disturbed by somebody whose personal timetable happens to be different from yours. Most staff and inmates also have a stake in the achievement of the institution's broad aims, whether it is to provide temporary or long-term shelter, nurture, or help to a better social adjustment; and the emergence of the appropriate regime is bound to be obstructed if the institution is constantly in a state of turmoil.

It would be easy to exaggerate this community of interests. Such was the view which was widely accepted in industrial relations in the 1950s; it was assumed that workers and employers had a similar interest in the prosperity of the firm, and that all labour problems could be solved by supplying the workers with more information about the firm's affairs and giving them some say in its decision-making. In fact these methods worked in only a few isolated and very special cases, and this was because the interests of workers and employers are not the same: there remain irreducible conflicts of interest between them. For the same reason one could hardly expect the resident of a preventive penal institution, incarcerated for an extended period because it was believed that he represented a danger to the public, to feel that he had any stake in co-operating with his gaolers, except in so far as this was necessary for his own comfort during his sentence. 'Doing bird', with the custodial compromise, which is its organisational outcome, is a very limited form of inmate co-operation. In other kinds of regime also, the staff (perhaps under public pressure) may feel that they had to insist on certain policies which inmates would never choose for themselves.

Apart from such structural incompatibilities of interest, residents may not always appreciate fully the value to them of some degree of social stability in the institution. Children may be more preoccupied with the play activity of baiting a member of staff, or with resolving their own group stresses by using him as a scapegoat. The long-term implications of their behaviour may be difficult for problem individuals, with their characteristic orientation towards here-and-now gratification, to grasp. Retarded individuals may not always understand. In other words, the underlying communality of interest may be there, but not be recognised as such.

It is to meet this common situation that practitioners like Homer Lane,[11] David Wills, and J. Edward Seel[12] have proposed varying techniques of inmate self-government. Wills argues that full self-government in the institution is hardly realistic; he proposes instead, what he calls 'shared responsibility' in which staff and inmates make decisions jointly. Certainly the staff, as representing the public, have a stake in what goes on in the institution; shared responsibility would seem the obvious way of acknowledging that fact.

Many community problems within the institution can be left to be solved by the machinery of shared responsibility — joint committees and meetings to analyse problems in the light of members' collective experience, and to work out and enforce solutions. In the process of dissecting what has been happening both inmates and staff come to recognise the validity of the solutions which emerge and to accept a commitment for applying them. The emergence of norms to this effect within the group-as-a-whole (see Chapter 4) becomes important in making this effective. Such an appraisal of the facts is of course an acid test which bogus solutions cannot possibly pass. As a result staff may sometimes have to abandon other prescriptions, possibly more convenient to them. The danger (especially where deep-rooted staff motivations are involved) is that they will then either want to bring the experiment in shared responsibility to an end, or to subvert it by manipulating the machinery behind the scenes. The latter would be no less fatal than the former to any hope of achieving a common commitment to the answer which emerged.

An example of this approach in operation is the way in which stealing was controlled in Woodmarsh,[13] a school for difficult children. As all the children tended to steal at times nobody benefited, and all suffered aggravation from it at one time or another: a classic example of the interest which all members of a community have in the maintenance of law and order. As long as the staff tried to suppress stealing unilaterally they had to reckon on the opposition or at least indifference of the children — always excepting the current victim. When, however, the staff explicitly withdrew from the situation, saying that it was a matter for the children, alien authority elements were eliminated. Discussion led the children to perceive that their true interest lay in controlling stealing — which of course being 'on the inside' of both the inmate world and the child mind, they could achieve more easily than the staff.

The social lesson is not always so clearly discernible. Where this is the case, it is permissible for the staff to bring about situations in the community to hammer home the lesson. It is the acid test of experience that matters, so that such action should not be stigmatised as manipulation. Thus when David Wills found his children losing interest in shared responsibility, he would take over for a time, and steadfastly decline even to consult them — in order to bring home to them by comparison the value of participation.[14]

There remain the residual conflicts of interest. It is better for the staff to admit these frankly than to pretend they do not exist, while trying to achieve their own ends by sleight of hand. The latter is inconsistent with the aim of basing law and order on an honest factual basis. Responsibilities in an institution do differ as between staff and residents, and this may make it necessary to set out the limits within which shared decision-making may operate. If residents find this difficult to accept, this must be an inconvenience to the staff, but it is also an opportunity to explain their role in the institution and how this affects the situation. If their explanation is then open to the same kind of factual analysis as other community experiences they may even learn something themselves about what their role in the institution does or does not require in the way of arbitrary power.

It is important nevertheless not to leave the impression that the role of authority in the institution is negligible. In an institution in a democratic society it must be open to challenge, but all of us, children or adults, are glad at times to have a parent or parent-surrogate to lean on. The authority of the father-figure is always great. The deputy-head of many an institution has ruefully discovered also how focused this can become, as he struggled to control the institution during the head's absence. Because of its appeal to the child in all of us, the staff member has an obligation to use his authority sparingly; dictators have always been able to use their symbolical significance to seize power for themselves at the cost of their subjects.

The use of personal authority should of course vary enormously according to the nature of the institution. Where, as with the preventive institution, the commitment of the inmates to institutional aims is minimal, it will play a large part. Where individuals have not, or have not yet, acquired sufficient self-imposed control, as with children, or retarded or mentally disturbed residents, it will be important both in order to support them in their attempts to discipline their impulses, and in the longer run to help them to internalise the necessary controls by identification with staff, so that external restraint becomes less necessary. But this latter is an aspect of Change to be examined in Chapter 7.

Chapter six

Relationships

This chapter is concerned with personal relationships, and more particularly with how staff relate to inmates. The assumption here is one which is basic to social work: that it is through his relationship with his client that the social worker can help. The client may need reassurance, encouragement, or support, in which case the social worker can attempt to communicate these attitudes through the personal bond between them. Alternatively, he may use the client's regard for and dependence on him as a lever to bring about changes in the latter's behaviour. But a relationship is a two-way channel of communication. Though the client may be influenced through it by the social worker, so may the social worker by the client.

Although all social workers are open to this kind of influence, social workers in residential care are more vulnerable than most others. This is partly because of the total institution elements present in all homes. It is not only the inmates who have to satisfy most of their human needs within the four walls of the institution. This is often the plight of staff too — especially if they are resident themselves. They are tempted to find objects for their emotions among other residents, and while one consequence of this is that personal relationships among the staff become very intense and often fraught, clients also get drawn in.

Staff may develop strong feelings about a particular client. They may like him, or dislike him, and they may not always be able to prevent this from affecting what they are trying to do for him. At the very least they will probably communicate their feelings to him through their personal contacts with him. Or they may identify with his problems so strongly that they can be no more objective about them than he is himself. Sometimes triangular relationships develop. Two members of staff may be rivals for the affections of a particular client, or special treatment given by a staff member to a client may be resented by another. Often situations of this kind can spread through the staff and inmates in ever-widening circles, and end up by having a deleterious effect on the work of the institution as a whole. Stanton and Schwartz describe just such situations in a ward of a mental hospital.[1] Such occurrences are more likely because some institution workers are themselves deprived, seeking a home, parents, children, somebody to dominate, somebody to protect, etc., through this kind of work.

Psychoanalysts have studied these processes. To the response of the client to the worker they give the name 'transference'[2] while the reciprocal influence of client on worker they call 'counter-transference'.[3] Much of the training of psychoanalysts, or psychoanalytically trained social workers, is aimed at giving the worker an understanding of his own particular blind-spots, in order to alert him to the ways in which he might become emotionally entangled with his clients, to their detriment. Such insight would be valuable also to the residential social worker, but short of that, two safeguards can be adopted. One is to try to avoid appointing to residential posts people who want this kind of work mainly to satisfy their own personal needs. Such needs are always present to some extent, and serve a useful function in motivating the social worker, but where they are the main motive they mean that the worker will be tempted to exploit the relationship with the client for his own ends, rather than (and indeed often at the cost of) those of his client.

The other safeguard is to break down the insularity of the institution as much as possible. Staff should be encouraged to make as many social contacts as possible among outsiders. The individual whose whole life revolves around the institution may be a devoted and self-sacrificing member of staff, but may also be a menace to the development of cool and workmanlike relationships within the home.

Relationships within a home are not often encountered, as they usually are in casework, in pure culture. They are almost always developed in solution with some daily activity within the institution. We have seen in the last chapter that the way in which physical care and order are maintained is often an indication of the way in which the staff look upon clients and their work with them. The message may be communicated to clients by the same route. Staff must always bear this in mind, in case their actions come to belie their words. Indeed actions do sometimes 'speak louder than words'.[4] To talk about feelings to some clients may be embarrassing and even appear fulsome, whereas a caring act may carry its charge of feeling less ostentatiously but no less powerfully. Discussion of such matters may be beyond the capacity of young or mentally handicapped clients, who can nevertheless recognise when somebody is trying to do something to or for them.

Relationships, then, are of primary importance in the work of an institution, and they have their relevance to each and every one of the broad functions of the residential community discussed in Chapter 2. In the case of the institution as an asylum their relevance is straightforward. A warm accepting relationship with those with whom you share your life is a *sine qua non* for happiness anywhere. It is more difficult to achieve in an institution because so many people live in such close proximity to one another without any of the mutual obligations either of kinship or of having chosen each other as companions. And because it is a total institution the same group do almost everything together — the man whose table manners put you off is still around in the day room after tea. There is no escape from the big boy who persecutes you; you and he are thrown together all day long in the activities of the institution. These very factors, which make it so difficult to maintain happy relationships in an institution, make the maintenance of such relationships even more vital.

Staff may be subject not only to the pressure which results from close proximity, but also an inmate population who are not going to progress much in social and personal competence. Incurables have so often been found to be curable after all, that it would be foolish to rule out all possibilities of improvement. Nevertheless in an asylum, the norm in practice is going to be at best the maintenance of existing levels of functioning, and in the case of, say, the elderly or the chronic sick, deterioration must be expected. In an achievement-oriented society like ours, this is very difficult for some staff to tolerate. They try hard to bring about improvement: 'Go on, you can do it if you try.' And when they fail, they become disillusioned: 'You're not really trying, are you?' Cynicism and indifference are then often the result.

Some people are so constituted that they cannot adjust to this situation. The reformative daemon which drives them could be used to good purpose in a residential community with a rehabilitative function, but can be a burden to them and to everybody else in this kind of institution. The acceptable alternative, however, is not the emotionally passive individual, who will certainly stir nothing up, but will also give nothing out either. The relaxed person, comfortable with himself, and not only comfortable with other people but one who gets positive satisfaction out of his association with them, is the ideal staff member for the asylum.

It should be remembered that residents often see more of domestic and other non-social work staff than they do of social workers themselves, so the kind of relationship the former establish with inmates is probably of special importance. Maintaining these relationships is a social work function, to be achieved not only by staff selection, but by helping non-social workers in the institution to understand the characteristics of the inmate population, and the particular aims which the institution has set itself. That will include helping staff to see passing annoyances and provocations in the light of these facts. Thus old folks can be unreasonable and crotchety, in which case they are probably going to remain so, whatever you do. To react to this by ill-temper or sulky withdrawal will not help. Neither will such a reaction do much harm if it occurs only occasionally, but if it becomes the usual response, it is not only bound to damage relationships with the old person concerned but to affect also the staff member's relationships with other residents. The keynote is to learn to relax, to tolerate, and to laugh off difficulties. The emphasis is placed on learning to do these things, because what is required is a long-term adjustment of this kind by the staff. To restrain yourself from erupting by sheer will-power may work for a while, but not over the longer periods during which relationships have to be sustained in this kind of institution. The cracks will eventually begin to show.

Much of what has been said applies equally to the institution, usually a penal establishment, set up to provide for the long-term, involuntary confinement of persons for the protection of the public. The reason for their lengthy incarceration should be carefully noted. It is not because a long period is required in order to rehabilitate them — though this rationalisation has been used in the past and attempts at rehabilitation might be made incidentally. Nor is it as a just punishment for their past actions, but because of something they *might* do in the future. It is in fact for the good of somebody else other than the prisoner (i.e. the good of the public), and should not therefore be any more onerous than it has to be. It is for this reason that the regime should, like that of the asylum, be as pleasant as it can be.

There nevertheless are differences between the two. The most important is the attitude of the media and the general public, who will constantly try to impart punitive considerations of an irrelevant retributive or deterrent character into the way the prisoner is treated. Also he will, unlike many asylum residents, invariably be returning to the free community after his period of preventive confinement is over, and steps will need to be taken to ensure that he is then no less able to adjust to life outside than he was before. As we have seen, long-term prisoners are often affected by a process of 'prisonisation', compounded partly of institutionalisation and partly of criminalisation. To adopt the tolerating attitude recommended for asylum staff would leave a clear field for the development of prisonisation, which would be neither just to the inmates, nor in the long-term interest of the public whom the sentence to an institution was supposed to protect. The regime will therefore need to be so designed as to provide antidotes against prisonisation, the most effective probably being to break down the insularity of the institution by admittin visitors and letters very freely, and for example, making as much use of outside functionaries and services (doctors, teachers, parsons, etc.) as possible. As might have been expected it is mainly the 'total institution' aspect which has to be reduced.

The short-term, 'holiday break' institution is similar to the asylum in certain respects. Here also reformist zeal has to be subordinated to the maintenance of pleasant ongoing relations. The difference is in the relatively short and temporary nature of those relationships. Residents are going to return to their own homes before long, taking up again the relatives, friends and activities they left behind when they began their temporary placement. It is therefore important that none of this back-home adjustment should be disturbed more than is necessary by competition from the institution. It is bound to have some impact, though it will be less than and very different from the prisonisation effects just referred to. Unless former residents live some distance away from the institution, they will often want to maintain some kind of contact for a while. To reject such advances is unnecessary and would be hurtful. They may also sometimes hark back nostalgically to their placement experience, and even use it as a bargaining counter in their own homes: 'Even in XYZ they let me do that.' As far as their more important back-home identifications are concerned, however, the staff should take care to leave them unimpaired.

So no matter how attractive, say, a child may be, the staff member in such a home must avoid assuming any quasi-parental role in relation to him. No matter how flattered a staff member may feel that another particular resident clearly prefers him to all the rest of the staff, following him around and waiting on his every word, he must remember that the placement is short-term, and that the establishment of any strong bond will be only a source of unhappiness to both parties when the association has to be brought to an end.

Such an attitude calls for a good deal of self-denial on the part of the staff. If they are going to be able to achieve this, they have as we have seen to be people whose lives are rewarding and full, and whose emotional needs are reasonably well satisfied. The person who is emotionally deprived, and who seeks compensation from his relationships with clients, may sometimes be so parasitic on them that he is not really suitable for residential work at all. The close relationship involved in living together with clients would be very difficult for such a person to resist. On the other hand some forms of emotional need may dovetail so well with the needs of certain kinds of client, that they become a genuine advantage. Thus the woman who needs children to love, could play a very valuable role in an institution intended for the long-term nurture of children. What is clear is that neither she nor others like her would be well-placed in a short-term institution of the kind at present under discussion.

The touch needs instead to be light and avuncular. The orientation should always be outwards, towards the client's home environment, rather than inwards to the institution. The client may need frequently to be reminded that he is going home on a particular date, and that life at home is, and must be, very different from that which he is experiencing in the institution. The staff must avoid the expression of more than conventional regret as his departure date approaches; it was something which everybody had been looking forward to from the beginning as the happy consummation to a none the less pleasant break in the home.

Something has already been said about the values which might be brought to the nurtural institution by somebody with strong parental needs, but it is doubtful in an institution of any size if such persons should constitute more than a small proportion of the staff. If they did the emotional atmosphere would probably be too intense: for example, possessiveness and rivalry on behalf of their children would probably play havoc with the general atmosphere of the home. All of which probably means that such people would probably be most successful in smaller institutions — which nurtural institutions should be in any case.

There are other, more moderate forms of symbiosis between staff and children which can be very useful in this kind of setting. Some people simply like children, and so can give them love without any great void needing to be filled in their own lives. Such staff may well have children of their own, which is a bonus. It means that they will be experienced in the ways of childhood, and in overcoming the stresses encountered in rearing children.

As with the asylum, the staff directly engaged with the children need not be social workers. There is an argument that they should not be, as this might detract from the spontaneity of their behaviour as surrogate parents. It probably depends on whether a child's separation from his home is intended to be permanent or not. If it is, the nearer his substitute parents can approximate to the attitudes and behaviour of real parents, the better. There will still be complications arising out of the facts that it is a home, that they are not his real parents, and that his real parents do also exist, so that social work support will still be required.

Permanent placements will probably be few. Usually the parents will still be very much in the picture. They may be visiting regularly or not. They may occasionally take the child home, sometimes even intending to keep him at home, but have to bring him back again. There may be attempts to arrange boarding-out or adoption for a child. These vicissitudes would impose great stress on individuals who had had very little training, and had become attached to a child in the expectation that they would be responsible for him for a lengthy period. Social work skills would be required to enable staff to deal adequately with the parents, and with the repercussions which the parents' behaviour had on the children. And understanding the situation as they did trained staff would have anticipated problems of this kind. Their own investment in the children would have been less absolute, and their ability to deal with their own feelings to that extent increased.

They ought also to be able to do this without reducing their commitment to the children to such an extent as to damage their nurtural function. Dr John Bowlby[5] argued that a young child needs a warm, continuous and intimate relationship with his mother or a mother substitute if he is to develop into a happy and well-adjusted adult. One does not need to become involved in the controversies surrounding the further implications of Dr Bowlby's work in accepting that basic proposition.[6] Most experienced workers with children would agree with the importance of such an early emotional bond (though some might want to include the father or father-substitute)[7] as a basis for further emotional growth. Feelings in the child having thus been awakened and directed gregariously towards other people, instead of being hugged anxiously to himself, he can allow himself to experiment (still of necessity, mainly within the family circle) in establishing relationships with other people. As he finds his feelings reciprocated he begins to feel a loveworthy person, able to go on to make overtures to a wider and wider circle of persons. Without such a sense of security he could neither take his background for granted as he needs to do if he is to move on, nor assume the risk of rejection by others which his uncertainties about his own worthwhileness would make him feel every time he considered attempting a new relationship.

But the ability to establish relationships is only part of that process of growing-up, which the nurtural institution has to facilitate. There is also the learning by the child of the norms of behaviour expected in the society to which he is to adapt himself. We no longer demand that children shall behave like little adults; they have to be given time to get their impulses and needs under control and to mould them into forms which society is prepared to approve. On the way, they will behave like children not adults. Those responsible for their social training certainly need to be able to make demands on them, so the children must care enough for them to mind what they think; this is a situation which is conceivable only where the emotional links referred to have been forged between the child and those caring for him. But the parents (or the staff of a home) need also to be able to empathise sufficiently with the child's difficulties in doing what is asked of him. To make too many demands too soon could end not in his confident assumption of adult roles, but in his becoming an inhibited person, who has been able to make the precocious adjustment required of him only by a colossal suppression of his own needs.

The inculcation of social norms does not consist solely of requiring sacrifices from reluctant young savages. It also includes a positive process of identification — of modelling oneself on people to whom one is attached.[8] If the right kind of relationships exist between a child and the adults in his life, he will model himself on them, warts and all. This is something of a responsibility, but is one about which reasonably happy adults who get on well with other people will not become too introspective.

The preceding is of course a gross oversimplification of the process of human socialisation,[9] but it is perhaps enough to indicate the kind of relational task which confronts all parents, and also residential institutions which undertake to replace parents in the nurture of their children.

The nurtural institution is trying to facilitate change towards maturity in its residents — a process of social education. The rehabilitative institution is trying to change what is already there, a faulty pattern of adjustment, rather than to fill a void — a process which might be called social re-education. This distinction must not be accepted too literally. A person being educated is never a *tabula rasa*; there is always some resistance from something which is there already. Even if the client is an infant with very little prior social training, there is, as Freud has shown, the resistance offered by his innate biological nature. But many children in nurtural institutions are deprived children who have had previous 'faulty' social training, so that there is a strong element of re-education as well as education in the task which the institution has to attempt with them. Conversely many individuals in rehabilitative homes (whether children or not) will have been deprived of maturing family experiences of various kinds, and will therefore have 'voids to be filled'. And problems of adjustment even in adults have often been defined solely in terms of a failure in maturation, i.e. in nurture.[10]

The difference between the two groups is going to be largely one of degree. How much resistance will the previous experience of the client cause him to offer to the educational influence of the institution? This does not mean that the difference does not matter. It conditions the approach which must be adopted towards the client. Nurtural attitudes aimed at encouraging growth in confidence, and the sublimation of self-serving tendencies into socially acceptable patterns of behaviour, will also be necessary in the rehabilitative home, but they will be accompanied, and often modified, by the steps which have to be taken to circumvent resistances to change.

Examples of the types of client involved will help to make the nature of the task clear. There is the delinquent person, or the drug or alcohol addict. There is the psychiatric patient. There is the physically handicapped or the educationally retarded person, whose previous failures have sapped his confidence. Delinquency, addiction and psychiatric illness all require change in social attitudes, which may sometimes be deeply rooted in emotional maladjustment. In the case of adults they will be further reinforced by long-standing habituation, and the fact that they form part of an integrated pattern of accommodation to the world, which, whatever its defects, provides them with some satisfaction. To break into that pattern by changing some part of it is to hazard it all, a risk which few clients will want to take without some inducement.

In order to change attitudes which are so deeply rooted, one of a wide range of possible professional approaches will be required, and all have their implications for the kind of staff-inmate relationship to be established. For example in the case of psychiatric patients some kind of physical treatment may be adopted (ECT, brain surgery, drugs, etc.). There was a time when such procedures were used without regard for the state of mind which they produced in patients. Nowadays it is usually acknowledged that pre-operative anxiety and possible post-operative trauma might mean that the treatment had been successful in achieving its specific objectives, but had left behind fantasies about the effect of the treatment on the body, or feelings such as those of inferiority or depression, which constituted a new problem for the unfortunate patients. So hard-boiled neurologists are being forced to recognise the importance of the right kind of reassuring relationship with patients, and the need for talking over their fears about the treatment both before and after. As technicians they are not always able to do this kind of thing themselves, and if expensive psychotherapy cannot be provided it falls to the lot of the social worker.

In some of the kinds of care referred to, however, 'talking treatment' is not merely an auxiliary to something else, but the main means by which change is to be brought about. Further discussion of the rehabilitative role of the residential social worker will be undertaken in the next chapter. But in order to be in a position to outline the kind of relationships required, it is necessary to open up the topic in this chapter.

Speaking very schematically, there are three kinds of problems to be tackled: (a) inner conflict between strong personal desire and socially acquired inhibitions, a conflict which sometimes amounts to

71

neurosis,[11] (b) character disorder[12] where there is a lack of inhibitions, leading to impulsive acts as urges are discharged in behaviour without much let or hindrance, (c) subculturally engendered deviant attitudes.

The conflicted type of personality is said to arise out of an over-censorious upbringing. The individual sees the attitude in his environment (particularly that of his parents) as demanding the abandonment of many of his most powerful urges. This censure appears to him to be so threatening that he cannot take time to try to modify these impulses into more socially accepted forms, but must repress them, i.e. become unaware of them. The self he acknow-ledges is thus delusory, and is constantly challenged by impulses which repression has robbed of none of their motivational force. So he has to adopt various psychological mechanisms[13] in order to preserve the repressions intact, and thus protect his self-image and his good relationship with his environment. The social work task is to give him the confidence really to 'be himself' in spite of ingrained (if unconscious) fears that he would be rejected or punished if people knew what he was really like. So initially, a high level of acceptance and tolerance is required, accompanied by constant pressure on him to explore his own nature. As he becomes aware of his own hidden motives, he can be helped to find a new *modus vivendi* between his new self and his environment. The social or personal difficulties (the delinquency, the addiction, the neurotic symptoms, etc.) which were by-products of conflict are then assuaged.

The character disorder may appear to be the result merely of lack of social training — an unbridled colt kicking over the traces. If it is so, it is not a character disorder, and presents a much simpler remedial problem. The character disorder proper implies a difficulty in responding to social training, which may arise out of genetic causes or early upbringing, or more likely a combination of both.[14] From the side of upbringing, there is said to have been a lack of those vital early familial relationships (discussed earlier in this chapter) which give rise to responsiveness to others, and suscepti-bility to social influence. Character disorders are very intractable, though there is some evidence that they can be helped, especially in certain kinds of group setting.

Because such a person does not establish personal relationships we are talking at this stage about how to set him on the road to involvement with others. This will require to begin with a high level of tolerance because persons who have internalised so few social restraints are bound to engage in persistent, socially maladjusted behaviour. Indeed some of this behaviour may be so extreme as to be dangerous, so that the tolerance has to be accompanied by safeguards. Of course if these safeguards mean that the tolerant attitudes are frequently breached, the effect of the latter will be nullified so it is better if control can be maintained by appropriate organisational or even physical re-arrangement within the institution. Simply to tolerate dangerous behaviour in safety may not seem much of an objective to set oneself, and it is only the first, if the most essential step. Tolerance combined with a warm and accepting attitude will, it is hoped, lead the client to establish a close bond with the staff member in question, and set in motion at last those missing early stages in socialisation. And once a relationship of this kind has been formed, it becomes possible for the staff member to exploit this by making quasi-parental demands on him for self-control and self-denial.

By comparison with such complexities, the processes of re-socialisation required in other cases seem very straightforward. The offender whose deviant attitudes have been inculcated in him by an upbringing in a high-delinquency area, or the demoralised slow learner, may have had his attitudes firmed-up by habit or the role they have come to play in the scheme of things as he sees it, but they remain socially acquired attitudes without any deeper significance within his personality — though the continuing influence on the delinquent of his own home community is another matter altogether.[15] But such social and educational failures do need patience and encouragement if they are to try again. It is within such a framework that the re-educational processes to be discussed in the next chapter are likely to be effective.

Most of the previous discussion about relationships has concentrated on the kind of contact which staff should establish with residents. The relationships between residents themselves have been largely neglected, and yet they could be even more crucial for their happiness and progress. After all most of them see more of each other than they do of any of the staff. The very fact that special attention has been given to an individual may provoke rivalry or jealousy in others. Yet as Wills[16] and others have shown, it is possible to develop within an inmate group a recognition of the need to relate to different individuals, with their varying needs, in different ways. This is an example of the changing of the norms of the group-as-a-whole in a way which is helpful to social work, as discussed in Chapter 4. The group character of residential work must never be forgotten. The social worker wants a climate within the inmate group which is generally supportive of his therapeutic aims, or at least not wholly opposed to it. Group resistances with their more continuous influence and the strong loyalty which they can command, unless countered, would certainly represent an almost insuperable barrier to the achievement of institutional aims.

At the same time, the idea of achieving a monolithic emotional climate is unrealistic, and if it could be attained would be undesirable. For one thing, inmate relationship needs, as we have seen, will differ. Also the private world of the inmate has many functions to perform. It can provide an occasional respite for individuals from the pressure for change, an arena for testing out new modes of adjustment, a source of solace and mutual support. Also, separated as one is in the institution from one's own community the inmate society can provide you with a peer group in which your indigenous culture, whether that of a child, a working-class person, a man or a woman, can be legitimated and preserved. This has further implications of value to the institution. Any changes which do occur are then within what is for you a realistic cultural context. To attempt to change people is possible; to persuade them in the process to divorce themselves from their normal social milieux without any other recourse, is not. It is the job of the social worker in both constituting the inmate group and intervening with it to ensure that such constructive functions rather than those of resistance are generated within it.

Chapter seven

Change

From its inception,[1] social casework saw the changing of the clients' attitudes as the very core of its mission. If individuals or families were in difficulties it was assumed that this was largely due to faulty attitudes on their part. There might be accompanying material privations — poverty, living in slums, etc. — but to help people to remedy these without dealing with the way in which they approached the tasks of life was considered to solve very little. They would be no better equipped to succeed than they had been before, and would soon be in further difficulties.

Not that caseworkers entirely ignored broader social conditions. That had become impossible after the 1880s, when the era of mass unemployment began. Till then it was possible to say that a poor man was so because he was too lazy to seek a job, but industrial capitalism had now produced a situation in which there just were not enough jobs to go round. This lesson was hammered further home during the traumatic period of massive global unemployment in the 1930s, so that by the hey-day of social casework, in the 1950s and early 1960s, there could have been few social workers who were not aware of the need for social reform as well as work with individuals. Thus Gordon Hamilton wrote in 1951: 'There are unmanageable factors in the environment which the casework approach will not make manageable; broad-scale reorganisation alone will bring them to terms.'[2]

So social workers accepted an obligation to engage in political or other action aimed at improving social conditions, even though most of the time they felt that they had to take the social conditions of the time for granted, and concentrate instead on helping their clients to cope with and adjust to those conditions, so as to make a satisfactory life for themselves nevertheless. The individualistic orientation which they adopted to this end is well illustrated by their attitudes towards the giving of material help. They saw it as apt to make people dependent, especially if they became simply passive recipients of help, handed out to them by the social worker, instead of being encouraged to take the necessary initiatives themselves. The emphasis was on strengthening the individual's ability to stand on his own feet — which in spite of the lessons of history, was bound to make social workers somewhat ambivalent towards material benefits provided by the state.

In order to be able to bring about change in individuals, the caseworker equipped himself with a psychoanalytically-based theory of human development, in which present, faulty modes of adjustment were seen as reactions to long-forgotten but still smarting early experiences within the parental family.[3] When the individual gained insight into this shadowy part of his history it was assumed to lose much of its power to shape his behaviour. For example an individual who was constantly kicking against authority might discover that this was due to his early (and now perhaps forgotten or 'repressed') resentment of the control exercised over him by his father. In rebelling against his boss, the police, or the superintendent of the home in which he lived, he was unconsciously rejecting the restraints imposed on him so long ago by his father. In order to help clients to discover such hidden reasons for their behaviour, caseworkers developed subtle interviewing skills. These could easily have become manipulative in character, a form of brain-washing, but as a profession, social work surrounded them by ethical safeguards designed to protect the client from this danger.

This approach to human social problems allowed the caseworker by the 1950s to have begun to lay claim to a highly-skilled role, very far removed from that of the amiable do-gooder, which was most people's conception of him. Social work had become an expert and exclusive profession, to be undertaken only by those who had completed a lengthy and highly specialised course of training, and giving social workers (as some felt) a vested interest in resisting any change.

It was therefore all the more surprising that when the challenge came to social casework, its resistance collapsed so soon. The controversy was sparked off in the United Kingdom by Barbara Wootton's famous book, *Social Science and Social Pathology,* which objected to the personal intrusion she felt to be inherent in the 'personal adjustment' approach to casework, as well as its reactionary character encouraging people to accept existing social provision instead of demanding something better. She argued that social workers should confine themselves to helping clients to take full advantage of their welfare entitlement within the structure of the welfare state. This argument was couched in terms hostile to professional social workers, and produced an angry response from them. Nevertheless the tide continued to flow strongly against them, and it is probably true to say that in social work training courses and among younger social workers the current trend is to think much more in terms of advocacy, welfare rights and social reform than of changing the individual.[4]

It is against this background that we have to appraise the role of the residential institution in seeking to change people. Was the former casework approach so utterly wrong? Or has the pendulum swung too far in the opposite direction?

There is absolutely no doubt that there are, among the clients of social workers, many who need help in 'sorting themselves out'. Material deprivations may play some part in causing their difficulties. Thus a mother committed to a training home for incompetence in coping with her home and children may be so because she has been overwhelmed by the problems presented by poverty, undernourishment, overwork, and a dilapidated house. But even if some of these social disadvantages can be remedied she may still need help involving personal guidance if she is to regain her confidence and learn new and more effective ways of running her home and managing her family. And it is always possible that a few were inadequate housewives anyway — mentally slow, or feckless — in which case the social work task becomes almost entirely one of personal casework.

As we have seen the institution has its own part to play in helping socio-economically deprived individuals. Children can be removed temporarily from sub-standard homes, while steps are taken to bring those homes up to the mark. Old people can be taken in and cared for, when they can no longer look after themselves. Special needs can be catered for in the institution which would have to remain unsatisfied in many poor homes. At the same time a portion of the population of homes have in some sense failed in adjusting to outside society.

The social adjustment problems of asylum residents such as the elderly, the chronic sick, and the mentally and physically handicapped are obvious enough; they are in such an institution because it is felt that, public attitudes being what they are, they are going to need long-term protection from the demands of life outside. The conclusion that they will never be able to adjust to non-institutional life is however a pessimistic one, which one accepts only with the greatest reluctance. Wherever possible one would work towards a return to normal society, signifying this intention by placing the individual in a short-term institution where there was bound to be pressure for a speedy turnover. The changes required even in such cases may sometimes need only to be in the client's home environment, e.g. the child or the old person removed from an unsatisfactory home, whom it is hoped to restore as soon as his home situation has been improved (perhaps with social work help), or when suitable alternative arrangements have been made. The resident may then need little or no help in himself, though it is rare that such prolonged, unhappy experiences leave people entirely unscathed.

In other cases there will be no doubt about the need for personal encouragement and guidance. Sometimes the need for social work will be secondary only. In cases like physical or mental illness, the occasion for placement (say, in hospital) would be the need for medical treatment, but the patient's response to treatment (for example, post-operative shock) or anxieties about his family, his job, or other social circumstances outside may call for the help of a social worker. The assumption is that there is a psycho-social element in most forms of illness,[5] and that dealing with these will assist the process of recovery. A number of patients suffering from the same condition, or experiencing the same treatment, may sometimes be more effectively helped as a group.

But a number of mental patients nowadays are restored to the community not 'cured' in any absolute sense, but with their symptoms controlled by drugs so that they can attempt to cope with life again outside the institution. It is then social adjustment *per se* which constitutes the whole aim of treatment, and the extent to which it is achieved is the criterion of success. Social work which helps to that end has become something more than secondary: it has become essential to what is rather euphemistically called the 'social cure' of the patient.

There are other kinds of case in which social maladjustment represents the main justification for residential placement, among them criminals or delinquents, addicts, problem children and neglectful mothers. Many of them will have been committed by courts but by no means all. Thus there are those mentally handicapped persons who display behavioural as well as educational problems. These have often escalated via the aforesaid vicious circle from initial mistakes by the client — the latter having themselves arisen either from his impulsiveness or his lack of understanding. Any of these adjustment problems may of course be worsened by institutionalising effects resulting from the placement itself, especially if the home is of the more old-fashioned, total-institution type.

Some contemporary deviance theorists[6] are opposed to personal rehabilitative work by social workers — what they call correctional approaches. Some like Dr Thomas Szasz[7] even question the validity of treatment for mental illness. The main reason given for these views is that behavioural non-conformity is in no sense due to a personal aberration within the individual, and therefore amenable to a therapeutic process directed at his motivations and attitudes, but to social processes of various kinds, notably labelling[8] and segregation;[9] operating in the following way. First of all, 'correctionalism' labels deviants while they are still not very seriously at odds with society, and this causes other people to see them in a different light. In the course of accommodating themselves to these changed expectations by the rest of society, a shift occurs also in their own image of themselves. Both situational pressures and changes in self-concept, therefore, cause them to live up more and more to the label. Labelling is also a form of segregation, separating them, in company with others bearing the same label, from more conforming members of society. As a result of the increase in the proportion of their social interactions which then take place with other deviants, their deviant tendencies are intensified. Physical segregation, as in placement in an institution, is not necessay in order to produce such an effect: a parent, for instance, will try to keep his 'good boy' from associating with a boy with a bad record. But residential placement with like-minded people is a most striking form of segregation. It can produce institutionalisation, and criminal or other forms of inter-inmate contamination, as well as the stigmatising ex-inmate label often assigned to the resident when he is discharged.

Stigmatising labels will persist as long as public attitudes to prisons, mental hospitals, etc. remain what they are, and social workers have some obligation to work for a more enlightened public opinion on these matters. Inter-inmate contamination is another matter altogether. It implies an inmate group which has been allowed to develop norms which are opposed to the purposes of social work, and represents a failure in the social work task. In any case, the risk has to be taken. For it will be clear from what has already been said that it is a need for personal and even psychologically orientated help which very properly brings many people into the residential community. A recognition of the problems resulting from labelling and segregation does not eliminate such needs, though it makes us more conscious of the difficulties we are going to have in meeting those needs adequately.

Another argument put forward by deviance theorists and others (including Barbara Wootton) is more tenable. This is that the correctional approach assumes that adjustment to 'society as it is' is a desirable thing. In other words it determines for clients the ends which they should seek to attain, instead of accepting that these are debatable and should therefore be left for the individual to decide for himself. Many see this not only as socially unjust: often it is society and not the individual which is at fault. To attempt to cure rather than to hold people responsible for what they do is also challenged as an offence against the rights and integrity of the individual: as implying that the deviant is not a person who can be trusted to make up his own mind, but as sick or misguided, and needing to be brainwashed by individuals of superior mental or social calibre.

These dangers certainly exist. They are particularly likely when methods of rehabilitation are used which do not call for the understanding, and the willing co-operation of the client. Some 'behaviour modification' methods for changing people are of this kind — though as will be seen, this is not necessarily always the case. Equally the use of casework or psychotherapeutic techniques can be manipulative if the client is not consulted all the way through. The solution is in the use of the concepts of client, and contract, as discussed in Chapter 3. One should not underestimate the influence which one person in a relationship can exercise over the other. This is as true of friendship as it is of the casework relationship. Identification and other unconscious processes are always powerful. Nevertheless, the ethical commitment of the professional social worker to voluntarism should ensure that equal participation is more of a reality in social work than in most other forms of human interaction.

Some reference has already been made to behaviour modification as a rehabilitative technique. As the name implies the aim is to change behaviour directly, rather than to attempt to do it indirectly by changing something called 'attitudes' — mental structures which cannot be observed and may not even exist. Behaviour modification depends on a theory of learning developed mainly in laboratory experiments with animals, though human subjects have been used from time to time. The contention is that human beings learn by a process of 'operant conditioning', in which their own acts bring upon them consequences which they experience as either satisfying or the reverse. If satisfying, the acts are 'reinforced', and become habitual — they have been learned. If the consequences are unsatisfying the acts are 'extinguished'; even the mere absence of a positive reinforcement will lead to 'extinction' in due course. Deviance is seen as due to faulty conditioning, the reinforcement of the wrong acts. Rehabilitation is achieved by bringing about the extinction of such acts and positively reinforcing instead a more satisfactory behaviour pattern. Eysenck[10] has argued further that a congenital inability to respond to reinforcement may cause some people to be incorrigible social misfits to the extent of persistent criminality, calling for special measures to increase their conditionability, but his view has not on the whole been supported by the research evidence.[11]

In developing a rehabilitative programme on this basis, two possibilities are theoretically open to us. One is to ensure that undesired acts lead to some sort of discomfort, say by associating them with an electric shock, or feelings of sickness (induced by the administration of an emetic). This is not the same as simply punishing the miscreant; the discomfort follows directly from the act without the intervention of a punishing person to whom motives for imposing the punishment can be imputed, destroying the direct cause and effect relationship between the act and its consequences. Followers of Professor Eysenck have sometimes adopted this method.[12]

Commoner nowadays is the approach recommended by Professor B. F. Skinner of confining oneself to the positive reinforcement of desired behaviour, on the assumption that undesired behaviour, being unrewarded, will be gradually eliminated.[13] The evidence shows that this does happen in time, if positive reinforcements are entirely excluded. Circuses have long found that rewards are more effective than punishments as a way of training their performing animals, and this view is supported also by experimental research in the psychological laboratory. This shows that conditioned responses established through negative reinforcement are more easily extinguished than those resulting from the more positive approach — indeed, may sometimes fail even to be established at all.[14] Both of these outcomes seem to be related to the fact that negative reinforcement is concerned with eliminating undesirable behaviour rather than establishing permissible patterns. The search for permissible alternatives is left to the subject himself, and unless he is offered possibilities in this direction by the experimenter his behaviour becomes disorganised instead of being organised in the required new way.

Residential care offers very special opportunities to the behaviour modifier because the institutional environment can be controlled to meet the needs of a programme of conditioning to an extent which would be impossible in outside society. Professor Skinner has himself provided a method for this, based of course on the more effective approach through positive rather than negative reinforcement. This involves what is called 'contingency reinforcement' through a 'token economy'.[15] A staff member enters into a 'contract' with an inmate whereby the latter's achievement of a specified training target automatically brings some predetermined reward such as a money bonus or a period of leave.

An opportunity arose in California in 1968-72 to carry out a controlled experiment in the use of these methods.[16] This was the Youth Center Research Project, in which two correctional schools for delinquent boys were set up side by side, by the Department of

Youth Authority of the State of California, one being operated on the contingency reinforcement principle, and the other on depth psychology methods derived from Eric Berne's writings on 'transactional analysis'.[17] The latter approach is different from that of orthodox psychoanalysis, not least in its concentration on current personal interactions and their meaning, rather than on prolonged exploration of the client's emotional history, but they are alike in directing attention to the feelings and motives behind behaviour, and helping the client to gain insight into the part which these play in his life.

In this respect, both are in conflict with contingency reinforcement, which is solely concerned with behaviour, and rewards only improvements in behaviour. In the Youth Center Research Project the device of a token economy was used. The institution operated by means of a network of contracts between individual staff and particular boys. For instance, agreement might be reached between a staff member and an isolated and depressed boy to reward the boy with tokens, which could be either saved or spent, for any success he might have in joining in social activities with other boys, or in offering a greeting to staff members arriving in the unit. A boy of poor academic attainment would be rewarded for reaching a particular pre-arranged milestone in classroom work. Each achievement would be the point of departure for another similar contract aimed at achieving a further and higher target.

The obvious first objection to this approach is that most of the experiments on which the theory behind it is based have been carried out with animals: both ethics and practicability have militated against much rigorous experimental work with human subjects. The device of the token economy, for example, does not provide the kind of crucial test which the experimenter demands; the results as we shall see could mean a number of different things. Also can conclusions from research mainly with animals be properly applied to human beings with their much more developed nervous system? In particular do we not have, with human beings, to go beyond an attempt simply to change behaviour, to the changing of the ideas which lie behind and determine the direction which behaviour takes? Experiments in what is called 'higher-order conditioning' are being carried out, but they are still in their infancy, and in any case they are limited by the behavioural form to which they must be confined by the experimental approach of the learning theorist. You cannot study the mental processes behind behaviour if you are forced to limit yourself to the observation of the behaviour itself.

There is a further more technical objection. It has been pointed out that absence of the reinforcer for a period of time means that eventually the conditioned response is extinguished. It does look as if the effects of training by this method will not long outlast discharge from the institution, if discharge means returning to the adverse environment which presumably reinforced the original unsatisfactory behaviour. This is on the assumption that the home environment remains unchanged; social or behavioural work with the home may be directed to changing the existing patterns of reinforcements.

It is also arguable that even if operant conditioning methods worked, they would be morally reprehensible in a free society. Behaviour modifiers try to change a subject without his necessarily considering for himself the implications of such a change. He implements it almost automatically because of the conditioning effect allegedly produced by the reinforcers used. This, it is contended, is an affront to his dignity as a human being, as well as possibly opening up the way to manipulating him into behaviour which was detrimental to his interests. Some people point to the wider political dangers implicit in behaviour modification techniques: that governments might use them to eliminate political dissent.[18]

Skinner has tried to answer some of these objections,[19] and some of them are also met by the device of the contract in the 'token economy', rather like that proposed in this book as a way of guaranteeing a client's acquiescence in any social work undertaken with him. Its limitation as it is applied in behaviour modification is that it focuses the attention of the subject solely on the relationship between the task and the reward. The ultimate aim, a more permanent change in his behaviour, possibly having widespread ramifications throughout his way of life, are not brought out, and indeed if they were, would complicate the simple association between task and reward which alone enables it to be seen as a conditioning process pure and simple, freed of any non-behavioural, deliberative mental activity. In the last analysis then, the token economy suffers like other behaviour modification research with human beings, from its essential behavioural character, that is, that it cannot take into account the individual's concept of himself: how he sees himself and his future, and how this affects his behaviour.

The value of an approach which does, is suggested by some of the differences found between the two schools in the Youth Center Research Project. Boys were distributed between them at random to ensure that both had similar kinds of inmate populations. It was hoped that any differences in the effects which they produced among the boys in their care could then be attributed to the differences in rehabilitative approach rather than to prior difference in the boys' own personal characteristics.

The results from both schools were sufficiently favourable to provide a convincing answer to those who say that residential institutions have no real part to play in social work which is aiming to bring about improvements in clients' social adjustment. The Youth Authority report points out that[20]

> a high proportion of the wards [i.e. the boys] became more socialised, less alienated and more responsible during their period of institutionalisation. They achieved scholastically at a high rate, and became more optimistic about their future. Most important, they were doing well on parole.

It should be remembered, of course, that both of these institutions were well-staffed, and operated on consistent treatment philosophies. There is no blanket vindication here of all residential homes, or even of the methods used in this experiment.

Both schools were successful then; but there were differences. The behaviour modification programme was rather more effective in reducing misbehaviour in the institution, and also showed higher gains for inmate independence, calmness and ability to communicate. The benefit derived by residents from being presented with a firm and intelligible set of social demands seems clear here. Perhaps also understandably, the more passive and conformist inmates benefited most.

The transactional analysis group, on the other hand, showed less anxiety and depression, a more favourable attitude towards themselves, and more optimism about the future and about their ability to keep out of further trouble after discharge. They had also a better attitude towards adults and authority, and more confidence that they had begun to resolve their personal problems, and could control their own destinies. Although performance on parole was similar for both groups then, there are differences favouring those subjected to transactional analysis, which appear to be concerned with their grasp of the life situations confronting them, and their readiness to tackle them. These suggest that there are advantages to be derived from trying to give people a greater understanding of themselves and their situations, instead of leaving the black box of motivation firmly closed and seeking instead merely to eliminate or establish behaviour patterns *per se.*

To close one's eyes in this way to possible processes going on within the client's consciousness does also leave obscure the real meaning of the changes which reinforcement appears to have brought about. Introspection would suggest that motivations (like cupidity for instance) are at work, and might just as well be recognised and exploited more directly. There is some doubt even as to whether it is the token rewards which are effective, or the relationship with and approval of the staff member concerned, approval which is symbolised by his giving his client a reward. The Californian experimenters themselves are in no doubt about the importance of the relationship with the staff. If they are right, then we are dealing with something complex in the way of interpersonal influence which calls for skill and sensitivity on the part of those who wield it. Acting as if nothing much is happening between client and worker may then be throwing away the most potent means which the social worker has for bringing about change.

What one certainly cannot leave out of account, however, in institutional life, is the importance of the group. This has a continuous and powerful effect on the behaviour and attitudes of all inmates, which probably reaches its peak within the inmate subculture of the prison, largely because of the way in which staff influence is excluded. Speaking of the similar situation in some correctional schools, Fritz Redl wrote of the ineffectiveness of therapeutic sessions where they had to operate against the resistance of indigenous group factors within the home. Referring to the American correctional school, he described how 'Several times a week the youngster is . . . exposed to the influence of a psychiatrist in interview contact, and is from there, sent back to a place where every wall oozes gang-psychological defence'.[21]

These group influences can be of various kinds according to the kind of population with which the home deals and the morale of its inmates. They may, like those in Redl's correctional schools, be resistive to the official aims of the institution, and deplorably effective as such because of the otherwise desirable group solidarity among inmates themselves. Or the group may act instead as a source from which apathy and pessimism spread among its members, giving the whole establishment a depressed and futile air. In an institution which has achieved some degree of unity and purpose, the group climate will be co-operative and helpful.

Usually group climate is ignored and its consequences in making the staff task harder or easier explained away as due to stupidity or cussedness on the part of inmates. Where the existence of group factors is acknowledged, as for example where the influence of 'bad elements' among the inmates is suspected, the answer is seen to be one of trying to neutralise its influence, by moving people around, 'leaning-on' particular individuals, or most commonly of all, increasing the amount of surveillance by the staff. None of these get to grips with the real issue, which is that as a human society, the residential institution will always generate its own social processes. Unless steps are taken to try to ensure that those processes are helpful to the social work aims of the institution, it will be a sheer coincidence if they are. Indeed they are more likely to be the reverse, in reflecting the common problems of their residents, or in reacting hostilely to the inevitable frustrations of institutional life.

We return to the proposition put forward in earlier chapters, that the human group is a powerful socialising force, and that social workers in residential institutions should be ready to make use of its potentialities in the interest of their clients.

What would be helpful would be if inmate groups were encouraged to examine in their groups the daily problems which arise for them in living together within an institution, and an institution moreover which has a particular aim in prospect. The reference to the aim of the institution is important; some of the problems encountered by inmates will be a result of that rather than simply arising out of community life as such. Security measures, regulations, food, work or other programme elements, are all capable of being perceived as 'a problem' by inmates.

The assumption is that the problems which manifest themselves will be problems of adjustment with which inmates had difficulty outside. They are now having an opportunity of gaining further experience in coping with these situations. It is true that they have failed in this task in the past, and now have the further handicap of established habits and attitudes which will have to be broken down if they are to do any better in the future. Nevertheless there are some factors on their side. All institutions, by their nature, are to some extent shut off from the rest of society. This means that they provide a pattern of community life which is simpler than life outside, providing clearer lessons from experience.

Indeed because the regime can be planned, it is possible to 'stage' lessons of this kind. Often by a minimum of environmental 'structuring'[22] the value of a particular social institution or mode of adjustment can be demonstrated. An example already referred to is David Wills's assumption of dictatorial power to demonstrate the preferability of the maintenance of order by inmates. Another was staff refusal to put down thieving in a school for difficult children, providing inmates as a result with a motive to do something about it themselves. In all such cases staff need to do more than simply take up the particular posture and then leave it to residents themselves to find their way out of the mire. Group discussion may produce a workable solution for them, but where necessary the staff themselves have an obligation to participate constructively in these discussions. One is reminded of the classic group experiments carried out many years ago by Lippett and White[23] in which 'democratic' ways of handling groups were found to lead to more progress than either 'autocratic' or 'laissez-faire' approaches.

Experience gained in the institution can differ helpfully in yet another way from that obtained outside. As a protected world it is a situation of reduced pressure as compared with normal society. You can make mistakes without suffering serious consequences as a result. When our jobs, our friendships, our families are at stake, few of us are prepared to take risks; we play safe and stay with the familiar no matter how dysfunctional this may have proved in other respects. 'Better the devil you know.' It is the job of the institution staff to ensure that there are no dire consequences for residents as a result of their mistakes, so that they are encouraged to take the risk of trying something new. This is bound to lead to some degree of permissiveness, of tolerance of unadjusted behaviour, and the balance between this and the very necessary framework of order and stability within the institution is a delicate one. It is bound to be a question of personal judgment, and will therefore be decided in most cases partly by an objective appraisal of the group situation in the institution, and partly by the kind of institution climate in which the particular staff feel that they can work and feel safe.

The emphasis is on stimulating and guiding the group's own self-directed activity. The staff member would encourage the group to tackle its problems, interpose questions, or even, if the group seemed to be getting 'bogged-down', offer possible solutions from time to time. Where individual or group anxiety had led to 'resistance' to the exploration of some aspect of the problem, he could help the group to discuss the reason for its reluctance. Otherwise he would devote himself to helping the group to marshal its collective resources of knowledge, experience and personality types in the interest of its members. These methods are well-documented in the groupwork textbooks.[24]

Two questions arise immediately. In all this talk about groups, are not the individual and his uniquely personal needs, not to mention his privacy, being forgotten? And is there no active role available to the social worker? Must he never be decisive? Is he doomed always to be a kind of commentator from the sidelines, the game itself being monopolised by the inmate group? After all it was these very components, the exclusive concentration of a social worker's personal influence on a particular individual client and his needs, which has been assumed to characterise social work, in the form of casework in the past.

There is no reason to believe that in working within the framework of a group, the interests of the individual inmate are going to suffer. Those interests will be greatly affected by the group anyway, especially in a residential context, whether the social worker works with the group or not. If he is prepared to involve himself with this process he has some hope of influencing it. But to see social work with groups as ignoring individual needs, is to see it as some sort of mass process, in which all are treated in the same way. This is not how it works. Instead there are a variety of highly personalised inter-actions between individual group members, as well (under competent direction) as a gradual increase by the group-as-a-whole in the understanding of differing personalities and differing needs. To put it in another way, the group provides a number of avenues to acceptance, while the individual casework relationship provides only one.

Privacy is another question entirely. There are, of course, sub-cultural variations in the demand for privacy: working-class clients are more willing to share experiences than the more privatised middle classes.[25] However, inmates will occasionally withhold matters which they consider to be of a more personal character from the residential group, and this is not only legitimate: it may be a precondition for personal growth in the otherwise rather public world of the residential institution. So there can be no rejection of individual interviews on the doctrinaire ground that such matters should be raised in the group. All such interviews will of course take place within the existing group framework of the institution, so that the social worker cannot ignore group pressures and possible group reactions. In this very real sense, individual casework does not exist; the group is always present, though in varying ways and to a varying extent. Nevertheless the form which its presence takes does make a difference.

Whether the social worker accedes to a request for individual attention, or tries to channel the problem back into the group, will depend on the nature of that problem. The way in which the resident sees the matter is of the greatest importance here, and this is influenced by the existence of a contract between him and the worker. But the social worker is not (as we have seen) precluded by this from exploring other (possibly unconscious) motivations such as a desire to avoid the more searching investigation of the inmate's problems, which is likely in a group rather than an individual setting. Sometimes the very effectiveness of social work in groups may cause some clients to fly from it to the less demanding setting of the individual interview. If this happens on a large scale, all the more emotionally-toned and significant material being withdrawn for individual attention, the group sessions (not the residential group as such) will become unimportant to residents, and die of a kind of emotional anaemia.

As was indicated in the last chapter, there are broad classifications within which the individual needs of clients can be subsumed, and these will have a decisive influence on the overall approach to be adopted by the social worker, whether in group or individual sessions. Thus there is the world of difference between the 'uncovering' approach required for the client whose problems arise out of inner conflicts, and the progression from tolerance to identification prescribed for the character-disordered individual. The former is aimed at relaxing over-rigid inner controls, and enabling the client to then find a modus between his inner world and the demands of society through the experience of a relationship with his social worker or the group. The latter has the reverse aim of inculcating inner controls in persons in whom these are lacking. Problems of subcultural origin, calling for a process of re-socialisation for which the groups seem particularly suitable, are still another variant.

The second doubt expressed about a group approach to the changing of the attitudes of residents has to do with the apparently self-effacing role of the social worker. But social work groups are not self-determining. The role of the social worker is important in posing questions, helping to give expression to ideas and conclusions towards which the group is fumbling, throwing light on resistances to progress which arise within the group. This was summed up in the idea, put forward in an earlier chapter, that the role of the social worker was in part to make up for the imperfect membership composition of the group itself. He has to be adaptable enough to substitute for missing personality types, missing forms of experience, and missing resources of knowledge.

But his influence does not end there. There is the prestige attached to persons in authority. Also the emotional dynamics of the transference cause him to be endowed by clients at times with personal characteristics possessed by figures important in their past, and therefore in their present problems (e.g. the attitudes of parents, siblings, a lover, or the embodiment of conscience or authority). This gives him great significance in their eyes. He can also utilise this manifestation to help them. He can point to it as concrete proof of the existence of particular problems within the group — or in the individual client, who relates to him in this way in the home. He can also help clients to work through and examine their transference behaviour, as a step towards understanding the problems out of which it has arisen. Incidentally the social worker himself will fully appreciate what is going on around him in the institution only if he can recognise that he is sometimes being invested by residents with fantasy qualities of this kind. Together with his special knowledge and his social work skill, these factors mean that in addition to playing a vital role in facilitating the group's own deliberations, he is going to have a very powerful direct influence on its work. This is why the idea of a contract looms so large: to help the social worker to resist temptations to manipulate clients towards aims which are his rather than theirs. This is a particular temptation in the residential institution where twenty-four-hours-a-day social work places great pressure on the staff. Residential staff are understandably attracted by solutions which make for a quiet life and an orderly home.

Chapter eight

Outsiders

The residential institution is a kind of 'social island': a community separated to some extent from the rest of society, and thus developing customs and relationships which are also distinct. The means of separation may be walls, locks and bars as in the case of a prison, close surveillance as in an institution for the subnormal, or personal dependence as with an old people's home, or a children's home. These insulators may differ widely in the extent to which they can be permeated, allowing movement from or into the institution, and therefore in the degree to which the way of life of the institution can diverge from life outside. In the traditional total institution, where the boundaries of the institution with outside society are strongly maintained, life may become very different indeed, and adjustment to it by inmates lead to an inability to cope with normal life. This is central to what is called 'institutionalisation'.

Recognition of this danger has led to various attempts to avoid it. Some of these involve reducing the amount of time spent in the institution, so as to minimise its effects; these have been referred to in an earlier chapter. Others seek to reduce the insularity of the institution itself, by increasing the opportunities for inmates to spend time outside the institution, or for visitors from outside to come in. The former would include home visits, expeditions (closely supervised if necessary, as in the case of handicapped inmates), going out to work or for evening visits to the pub or the cinema. Even the most total of all total institutions, the prison, has been affected by this trend. Not only have open prisons[1] been developed for low security-risk prisoners, but even the walls of closed prisons have been breached to some extent. Hence home leave and work outside the gates, and the development for long-term prisoners at the end of their sentences, of hostels[2] within the prison grounds from which men go out freely during certain hours for work or recreation, though subject at other times to the authority of the prison.

Something needs to be said at this point about the day centre.[3]

Clients sleep at home, but attend at the centre each day, usually taking a midday meal there. The range is wide, including day nurseries for pre-school children, day hospitals or clubs for the elderly, psychiatric patients, etc., and day training centres for offenders or the mentally handicapped. A centre, according to its purpose, can provide education, vocational training, medical care, or even the shelter or the daily support of a disciplined environment which it is felt that certain classes of client require.

It may be physically contiguous to the corresponding residential institution — like certain day hospitals, which form part of a larger hospital complex. Such a location has advantages, in that it enables the day centre to make use of the resources of the parent institution (in the case of a hospital it could be prohibitively expensive to provide these separately), but it also means that any stigma attaching to the residential institution itself may rub-off also on to its satellite day centre. Thus a psychiatric patient may be reluctant to attend a psychiatric day centre if it means risking being seen going through the gates of the mental hospital. There is also the danger of the day centre's being contaminated by institutionalising influences emanating from the residential institution. The sharing of staffs, for example, may result in the development of similar attitudes in both establishments.

This outcome is particularly likely if the day centre is used (like the hostel) as a half-way house on the road to independence for discharged institution inmates. Then the dependent attitudes of the clients is reinforced by the institutionalising behaviour of the staff, especially if the two had a previous relationship of the same kind when the client was living in the institution. In fact day centres are not often used in this way, but usually as an alternative to some form of residential care. From this point of view they enable the client to maintain his personal and social relationships in the community, and to preserve his social skills intact. Incidentally, the elimination of the residence factor also means that costs are greatly reduced: the capital cost of providing sleeping accommodation, and the recurrent expense of night-time care and supervision, and of employing staff to ensure effective containment are all saved.

Nevertheless there are many parallels. Regimes need to be developed for attaining the centre's objectives, and these objectives may fall into some of the classes referred to in Chapter 2. Daily programmes have to be implemented. The client group in a day centre will often gain as much cohesion and influence as its counterpart in a fully residential setting (especially if it remains together as a group for a while), and can be handled in such a way as to either obstruct or facilitate the realisation of the social work aims of the centre. And like the institution its preoccupations are going to arise out of the daily experiences which clients share with one another in the centre.

Working in a day centre ought not, of course, to be as stressful as in a residential institution. There are opportunities of getting away from the job and the clients when the day's work is over. And staff can maintain for themselves a full range of outside interests, and so are less likely to become institutionalised in their own attitudes and therefore institutionalising towards their clients.

There is no doubt about the value of innovations such as those aimed at opening up the institution to outside influence; the institutionalised person is handicapped not only in any subsequent attempt to resume his life outside, but even (in the case say of asylum residents) of assuming normal self-dependent roles inside the home. However, the features of institutional life which have this effect, do so in part by virtue of their 'protective' nature, shielding people from the cold winds of normal life. If this kind of dependence is continued for long enough, it may make serious inroads into their ability to stand on their own feet, but for a time it can provide them with a respite from pressure and a simpler life-style. Personal confidence and social skill can be more easily built up under these conditions, but of course the demands made on inmates must then be gradually adjusted upwards if they are eventually to meet the more challenging climate of non-institutional life.

A policy of encouraging residents to spend more of their time outside the institution can be made selective in this sense. The amount of exposure can be graduated to the individual client's ability to sustain it and benefit from it, and presumably increases gradually as that ability increases so that discharge into the community is only the last step in a continuous process of social reconnection. It is a process which is focused on the social needs of the particular client, rather than on the regime as such. Nevertheless if a number of residents are spending much of their time outside the institution, they are bound to bring some of the flavour of outside society back into the institution with them. The whole point is to reverse any trend towards institutionalisation in the personal development of these individuals, which means if it is successful that they will come to appear as odd-men-out, imposing some strain on the home's inward-looking ways. And quite apart from any generalised influence like this upon them, many of their more specific experiences while 'out in the world' will be brought back with them as incidents to be recounted and in other ways, and have their own effect in directing the attention of other inmates outwards.

More likely to have widespread effects in reducing the general level of introversion within the institution is a policy of encouraging visits from outside. This means not only encouraging visits to inmates from their relatives and friends but also freer movement within the institution for members of the public, and doctors, dentists, teachers, tradesmen, etc. This will often be resisted by staff on the grounds that visitors get in the way of the work that has to be done. This is the argument which used to be (and sometimes still is) presented for restricting visiting-times in hospitals, but more and more hospitals are recognising the value of generous visiting arrangements. In other kinds of institution, where questions, for example, of hygiene or of keeping the decks clear in case of emergencies, are not as relevant as in hospitals, there is even less justification for the limitation of visits. To subordinate the social work task of an institution to administrative convenience is to allow the tail to wag the dog. Administration exists in order to make a success of that social work task and not vice versa.

Sometimes these intrusions from outside are resented however just because they fulfil the function for which they were intended. They cause residents to be more outward-looking, and therefore to be less well-adjusted to the institutional environment. They are said to be 'unsettled' by the visits. This used, for example, to be an argument used against frequent visits by parents to their young children in hospital. They would cry a lot afterwards, and show other signs of disturbance like bedwetting, fretting, sleeplessness and difficult behaviour. Following the pioneer researches of James and Joyce Robertson,[4] however, it became clear that whatever problems such reactions might represent for the staff, they are a good sign as far as the child is concerned. They mean that his feelings and his social interest are still active. The quiet behaviour of the 'adjusted' child is often a form of apathy, of withdrawal from feelings, with ominous implications for his subsequent development. 'Unsettling' the institution resident may be the last safeguard we have against institutionalisation.

The example of the young child in hospital underlines the special importance of maintaining contacts between the resident and his family. Even if he is unlikely ever to leave the shelter of the institution (as in the case of certain elderly or severely handicapped persons) such contacts will usually be important to him. Being in touch with your family is important for your sense of identity; you are not an almost anonymous resident in an institution, but a person with a place in a family and in the community outside. To feel that there is somebody who cares for you is also important for your sense of personal worthwhileness. All this quite apart from the break in the institutional routine, and the breath of outside air, which such contacts can bring with them.

Some visits by or to a resident's family can of course be damaging but even where this is suspected to be the case, much can be done through social work to help families to relate to their inmate relatives in a more helpful way. Even where relationships in the past have been bad, short periods of contact can often be tolerated by both parties without too much stress, and when they find, to their surprise, that this is the case, it can often become the springboard for better relationships between them. But in the end, it is the wish of the client about maintaining the link which must prevail. The social worker may have his own views about its desirability, and would be justified in expressing his views so long as the last word remains with the client. The only exception may be pre-adolescent children, though even here the child's objections must be given full weight when the decision is made. Unfortunately homes (especially for children) are often located in rather inaccessible rural areas, making it difficult for even willing relatives to visit, and providing a convincing alibi for those who do not want to be bothered.

There is a common danger against which staff must be fore-warned: that of becoming possessive about residents, and therefore jealous of their families. This is a special danger in institutions for children, especially where staff are themselves childless, but it exists also in other kinds of home. It is part of the value of residence that it evokes from staff quasi-parental feelings about residents, and puts these to good use. But seeing yourself as a good parent, and recognising the obvious shortcomings in the homes of some clients, it is fatally easy to reason that a resident is better kept away from his family. It is sobering to recognise that assuming such a responsibility brings with it a lifelong obligation to the client. But as has been said before, the largest proportion will return home some time anyway, and must be given the opportunity of getting used to the worst that their families can deal out to them. Nothing is gained by keeping them apart. If a bad home has been improved, regular and increasing contact can make that reassuringly apparent to the client, and also enable him to adjust himself to the new situation in his home while he still has access to the support and guidance provided by the institution. It will also enable his family to reacquaint themselves with him. If there are still undesirable features about the situation, both parties may have a need for time and help to accommodate themselves to what must be borne when he is discharged.

Some clients will need further help after they have been returned to their homes. Something has already been said about the need to remove the conditions in the home which made the residential placement necessary. This cannot always be done while the client is away, as it often involves a readjustment of attitudes between him and his relatives. If there have been regular visits to him by his relatives while he was away, or regular home visits on his part, this process, as we have seen, will have begun. But it will still acquire quite a different character when both know that they are being reunited on a permanent basis. No longer can they buoy themselves up for a short period, knowing that relief will not be long delayed. Sometimes, the placement itself will have made reunion more difficult. For instance, a mental patient may have been taken into hospital after a display of bizarre behaviour at home or among his friends. Their image of him, and their expectations of how he will behave on his return, will have been affected by this. And his behaviour on discharge may in truth be different from what it was before his illness, and produce its own response from other people; some traces may still remain of his mental illness. There may also have been changes in his own self-concept, how he feels about himself as a result of having been mentally ill. There are also possible institutionalising effects, if hospitalisation has been prolonged.

His task of adjustment has thus become quite a difficult one, and it would be callous to leave him to cope with it without social work help. If he were left to his own resources in this way, the scene would probably be set for a familiar vicious circle, in which perceived rejection by his friends and relations leads to withdrawal and hostility on his part, producing in its turn intensified rejection from others and eventually failure in adjustment. The whole process might well then feed back into his residuary mental difficulties, perhaps necessitating a return to the institution. It is easy to understand how similar problems might be encountered also by a patient who is returned home after an operation, especially if it has involved an amputation, or has resulted in some major change in his appearance or his mode of physical functioning.

The important requirement is always continuity between what was being attempted with and for clients during their period of residence, and what happens to them afterwards. It is this which has led to the contention that after-care should be the responsibility of the staff of the home, who should know the client well and therefore be in a position to continue his progress, rather than social workers outside, like fieldworkers of the Social Services Department, or probation officers in the case of ex-prisoners. Such a solution has been rare, largely because of the availability of fieldworkers with their special skills and contacts. But if institution staff could be involved in after-care in some way, it would provide some inoculation against that introversion out of which many of the disadvantages of residential care arise.

The disadvantages resulting from lack of continuity will loom larger as current trends towards what might be called 'intermittent placement' continues. This kind of placement is commonest in hospitals, particularly in mental hospitals. Mental patients are helped to control their symptoms with the aid of drugs, and then sent home until their difficulties build up again, when they return to hospital for another instalment of treatment. Such a policy is unworkable unless the various professionals involved with the patient develop a pattern of very close, long-term co-operation. One way of doing this is by forming a treatment team which unites the doctor, and nursing and other residential staff, who are treating the patient in hospital with the GP and the social worker responsible for him during his spells at home. This means that whether at home or in hospital he has the same doctor, nurse, and social worker every time, so that they know him and his illness, and he knows them. It also ensures that they are committed to working together as a group in implementing the agreed treatment programme for him.

The principles embodied in the idea of the treatment team are as valid for other groups of intermittent residents as they are for the mentally ill. Continuity of care and the familiar face are just as important, for instance, to the chronically ill or disabled person as he shuttles back and forth between his home and the institution. And in the case of the old lag it is probably only the return to contact with somebody who knows him only too well which is going to make it possible to break into the vicious circle of self-deception which has brought him back to prison so many times before.

There is much also to be said for some occasional exchange of jobs between field and institution staff. The advantage to the institution of involving its staff with work in the community, like after-care, has already been mentioned, but it would also enable both sides to appreciate better the particular stresses and difficulties of the other's work. Nothing is more likely to oil the wheels of co-operation, or to make for a more seamless joint between what happens to the client inside and outside the institution. The probation service have had staff in prisons as welfare officers for a long time, and have also taken prison staff members for attachments with probation officers, but Social Services Departments still have to be convinced of the value of an innovation like this, disturbing as it would be to both bureaucratic routines and the established pecking order in social work.

Although home and family are the most important of the outside relationships which need to be kept alive, they are not everything. The modern world is always changing, and the inmate who has been out of it for years may feel lost and afraid, even at the *prospect* of going out. This accounts for the phenomenon of what is called 'gate fever' among many long-term prisoners as they approach their discharge date. Many of them display anxiety as the time gets shorter, and may even get into trouble, apparently with the idea of losing remission. Of course, this kind of reaction is a result of institutionalisation — of preferring the institutional adjustment, which he knows and has learned to make successfully, to the unknown terrors of non-institution society. If the institution had been more open (in both directions) throughout his stay, his adjustment would have been less institutional, and the outside society would have been both less unknown and less terrifying.

He would also find himself better equipped to deal with the problems actually confronting him when the doors of the institution closed behind him. Quite simple things otherwise can seem impossibly difficult — like going into a café to eat, or handling fragile table china, after the more robust equipment of the home. A prison officer[5]

> described how an inmate at the end of a 15-year sentence had been taken out by him to Bristol city centre; the inmate was almost totally paralysed by the traffic conditions prevailing in the city, and clutched the officer's arm, imploring him not to go away for a moment.

It is important of course that these wider influences as they impinge on individual inmates, or on the norms operating within the institution, should be brought within the ambit of the social work process. What this means for individuals is that a client's feelings about his visitors, or about his own forays outside the home, will be open for discussion between him and his social worker. He has after all, not only to feel the impact of these experiences, but also to learn from them: to internalise them, and to cope with any difficulties which he may have in accepting or understanding them. But because all of these aims are really variants of the central task of social adjustment, they will often be best achieved through group discussion, that is through the deliberative process, discussed in the last chapter, which is intended to elicit and drive home the lessons of experience. Social learning is best attempted in a social setting. These new experiences will widen the group's 'range of induction',[6] providing learning opportunities for the member directly concerned, but also giving other members the chance of discussing his difficulties in coping with problems which they may all have to confront one day. But as we have seen, ideas are introduced to other members and indeed to the regime, which bring a premature taste of the outside world into the protected world of the institution, and this may produce its own problems. The lessons learned will, of course, depend on the characteristics of that outside world within which the resident gains his experience. Thus the practice of locating institutions in fairly isolated rural areas does not facilitate the learning of lessons relevant to life in a great city.

Problems for the residential community itself as a result of these incursions into its privacy will arise naturally for consideration within the same group setting: probably in the course of discussing the same specific experiences. Are visits disturbing the routine too much? Do people find it difficult to settle down in such an atmosphere of 'coming and going'? Is there a belief that some are so unsettled by their home visits that they mar other people's peace and quiet? It is out of debates around such issues that the new non-institutionalising climate will have to take shape.

Outside relationships are important for the institution in another way. No matter how impermeable may be its boundaries with the surrounding society, it will still have neighbours, who will feel that they are affected by its having come among them. At the very least they will probably feel that the amenities of their locality, and probably the value of their property, has declined as a result. And of course, even the most stringent controls over inmates' movements will not convince some of them that they or their families are not in imminent danger of attack or contamination from them. These are the usual objections put forward to the opening of a new hostel or home, especially in a middle-class neighbourhood. Even if relationships do get off to a bad start in this way, the institution has an interest in encouraging a more friendly attitude among its neighbours.

But in seeking to achieve this it must avoid doing violence to its own aims. The pressure from outside society is still for institutions to fulfil a containment function. People would prefer not to have offenders, the mentally ill or subnormal, or noisy, deprived or difficult children about on the streets, and this is especially true of those who live close to the home itself. It is tempting to try to avoid causing offence by restricting the movements of residents more than would be desirable, rationalising this is necessary for the maintenance of good community relations, and therefore in the long run in the interest of the institution itself.

Without thus selling its soul the institution is in no position to guarantee to its neighbours that their lives are not going to be affected by its activities. The very logic of encouraging residents to move around in normal society, making relationships and improving their social skills, implies that they will come into contact with other people. And because of the social difficulties which led to the placement of many of them, these contacts will sometimes be stressful for both parties. To be overly reassuring in negotiations with neighbours, glossing over these possibilities of friction will only lead to disappointment and anger later on, with the consequent danger of even greater pressure to take restrictive steps being brought to bear on the institution.

Such measures are in any case likely to be self-defeating. An iron curtain does not only keep inmates in; it also prevents a realistic picture of the institution and its population from percolating out. Fantasies about what goes on in the place are stimulated by draconian security measures ('They wouldn't do it unless it was necessary') and remain uncorrected by a knowledge of the facts. Thus the average man's picture of what mental patients are like tends to be very wide of the mark. They are usually seen as people who have lost control of themselves: raving and dangerous, or suffering from bizarre delusions. Few see them as they really are: sick people, often unhappy and confused, but perfectly capable of managing their own lives much of the time. When objective information is lacking, the way is open for people to project on to the institution all sorts of characteristics which it does not possess but which reflect impulses or fears of their own.

The more open the institution then, the more danger there is of friction between it and its inmates, and members of the local community, but also the greater the likelihood of its neighbours developing a realistic understanding of its aims, and therefore of the reasons why it is organised in the way it is. However, if understanding is to develop into sympathy and support, the connection between the two needs to be closer than is implied simply by a policy of welcoming neighbours into the home, and encouraging residents to go out into the locality.

Neighbours need to be involved as much as possible in the work of the institution. That they should be strongly represented on its governing body goes without saying — and these should be grass-roots local residents whose views are influential with others in the area, and not simply big-wigs. But there are also many other activities with which they might be encouraged to help, including fund-raising, visiting or occasionally taking-out inmates who have no friends or relatives of their own, running classes or clubs for residents on subjects in which they have some expertise, and organising occasional events like fêtes, parties, etc.

There is sometimes a feeling that if an institution is unsure of its acceptability in an area, it should keep a low profile. So one decides on a policy of containment: to be seen and heard in the neighbourhood as little as possible. This, it has already been suggested, is a mistaken policy. Similarly it is a mistake to believe that opposition will be allayed if as few demands as possible are made on the other local residents. All that this ensures is that local residents have no sense of commitment to the institution. To get them involved, to encourage them to contribute their time, talents and money to the place makes them feel part of it. Research with groups since the Second World War has shown time after time how participation in group activities leads to this kind of ego-involvement. And the more people have invested in the enterprise, the more stake they will feel they have in its future.

This ought not to be seen as a kind of trick, by which unsuspecting neighbours are drawn into an unwanted involvement, from which they cannot then escape. It is not as easy as that, and if it were it would be self-defeating. As the old saying goes, 'One volunteer is worth two pressed men.' So though the staff will need to explain and even 'sell' their ideas in the neighbourhood, it must not be by distorting or concealing the truth. To do this would be to frustrate the aim of improving local knowledge of the home and its aims and methods, the kinds of people it deals with, and the problems it faces, on which all its hopes for a supportive local community must rest. In any case subterfuges of this kind would be precluded by social work ethics. In so far as this persuasion is to be seen as a social work activity, it must be subject to the same professional constraints as work with clients, which means that the idea of contract applies here too.

As is also often the case in work with clients, any influence exercised will probably be mutual. Neighbours cannot participate so actively in the management and the programme of an institution without exercising at least some influences over it. Purists may feel this to be regrettable: the pure milk of institutional policy or nothing! This is unrealistic. The institution has to find a socially acceptable niche for itself, if it is to be more than a brief, bright display of fireworks. Only too many promising experiments in residential work have been short-lived because they failed to acknowledge the truth of this. That niche may be in part carved out by the institution itself; it may to some extent create its own favourable public opinion. But to remain obdurate in the face of all demands from either one's neighbours or society at large is not only a recipe for disaster, but may actually mean missing some opportunities for learning from other people who see your problems from a different point of vantage, notably an inevitably disturbing but possibly reinvigorating non-institutional viewpoint.

The importance of social considerations as these are not often recognised by the staffs of residential institutions. Juliet Berry[7] found that only four out of forty-four children's institutions which she studied were considered to be well-integrated with the local neighbourhood, and thirty-one (70 per cent) were somewhat isolated in the area.

The image of an institution in society at large (as distinct from the local neighbourhood) is marred usually only by very unorthodox behaviour, and some experimental institutions will want to take this risk. Much depends on the way in which any incidents which occur are dealt with by the television and the press. Hostility from powerful formal organisations in the wider society is another matter altogether; pressure groups (religious or welfare organisations, political parties, trade unions, etc.) usually know exactly what axes they want to grind. They can, however, normally present a serious challenge only if they are able to exploit the communications media, or gain the support of the employing organisation (usually a local authority or a voluntary agency) or the responsible government department, such as DHSS, DES, or the Home Office. Dissentient members of staff may sometimes seek support from an outside group of this kind, but the problem for the institution in such a case is an internal rather than an external one.

Pressure from the employing organisation has much more serious implications, as is so also with pressure from a government department which has inspectorial or grant-giving powers in the field in question. It is not really possible for an institution to operate for long on general policies which are defined as unacceptable by its parent organisation. This is as true of voluntary as of state agencies — indeed some voluntary bodies set up by special interest groups (for example, particular religious denominations) may circumscribe the activities of a home even more than a local authority. The kind of moral values on which a home and its programme are based is a case in point. And many of the larger voluntary agencies are enmeshed in just as much red-tape as any government or local government department.

Policy issues apart, however, the institution needs to find itself as much scope for free movement as it can. The infusion of profession-ally trained staff into Social Services Departments in recent years has shifted the balance of decision-making in local authorities from elected representatives to senior staff, and they are often now as prepared as the senior staff of the voluntary organisations to provide the 'cover' necessary to enable operational staff to operate with some degree of professional autonomy. There will be limits of course, and these will be set where it is felt by the employing organisation that agency policies are being breached. There is really no hard-and-fast way of distinguishing such policy issues from the rest. It is largely a question of how a particular issue is defined by the agency, and that may vary from time to time according to the political climate or public reaction. The important thing for the home is to try to establish that any departure on its part is a matter of detail, and not of policy. Of course many detailed changes will eventually add up to changes in policy, which indicates a strategy for those institutions which find the policies of their parent agencies a constraint over the performance of their social work function.

Public and political pressures are going to be important also in shaping the supervisory activities of government departments, but these activities will be influenced also by the currently received wisdom on the topics in question in those departments. These policy assumptions may sometimes have emerged out of the technical knowledge available in a ministry, but may in other cases be little more than current fashions which have come to be accepted almost as an article of faith. Some would argue that the post-war passion among HMIs for the more informal methods of education in primary classes is of the latter kind. An example of the irrational behaviour into which an inspectorate may be led by public clamour on the other hand was a decision some years ago by the then Ministry of Education that residential special schools for maladjusted children should not contain mixed populations of adolescent boys and girls, though an inmate group including adolescent girls and pre-adolescent boys was permissible. As one pioneer of these schools then remarked, the Ministry seemed more alarmed at the prospect of pregnancies than at the possibly less obvious damage which a disturbed teenage girl might do in her dealings with the younger boys.[8]

There is probably not much point in fighting government departments over minor issues, but in a pluralistic society we have to stand firm against undue centralising tendencies over major matters. The wise institution will then enlist its parent organisation in its support. Residential institutions are particularly open to threats from this quarter because they are concerned with developing their social work as part of the process of living together and often the two tend to interact on each other. Giving children some responsibility for their own behaviour may mean that for a while conventional standards of personal hygiene or institutional tidiness may not be maintained. For such reasons as these a predecessor of DES enforced the resignation of the head of a residential school; and a local authority (in an inspectorial not an employing role) has more recently attempted to close a London day centre for battered wives.

Chapter nine

Programmes

Social workers in residential communities are distinguished from most social workers outside by (among other things) the fact that they do have to concern themselves with developing a daily programme for their clients. There are, of course, some non-residential social workers, in youth clubs, community centres, day centres, etc. where the programme provided for clients is the very essence of the social work task. But generally speaking, social workers employed outside of homes can take for granted a range of activities and relationships, provided by a large number of groups and organisations, and can make use of these as their work requires. Thus a caseworker who feels that a subnormal client might benefit from training in basic social skills can find a training centre for him, and a lonely old person can be encouraged to join a pensioners' club.

In conformity with the aims of reducing the insularity of the residential home, maximum possible use should be made of these outside resources by the residential social worker also. Hostels from which residents go out to work or school during the day, and to clubs, pubs, bingo or dances, etc. in the evening probably approach nearest to the ideal in this respect. Yet at the very least, even they will have collective arrangements about meals, sleeping arrangements, etc. to make, which form an essential part of the daily routine of the hostel, and take the form they do because this is a hostel and not a family home.

In other cases it is the need to 'temper the wind to the shorn lamb' which necessitates more extensive institutional provision. Inmates who cannot cope with the outside, such as some elderly or mentally handicapped persons, or some whose needs are such that they need a special kind of provision, such as the maladjusted schoolchild who truants or is unmanageable in the ordinary classroom, illustrates what is meant here. Generally speaking the emphasis is on 'sheltered' provision, though one must also take note of the explicit containment motive in penal institutions, where the need for a programme arises out of the requirement of the law that inmates shall be incarcerated rather than out of any need of inmates themselves.

These distinct kinds of activity can be found in the daily programme of an institution: (a) the satisfaction of residents' routine needs, (b) recreation, (c) purposive activity. The difference between the last two may not be clear without further explanation. It rests on a distinction made by Karl Groos[1] between play and work. Play he sees as an activity which is enjoyed for its own sake, while work has some purpose outside of itself. The word 'recreation' is used here in the sense in which Groos used the word 'play', and is contrasted with those parts of the programme of a home which have some purpose outside of the pleasure of the activity in itself. Such purposes might be for example to improve residents' social skills, or to help to maintain order within the group. They will clearly reflect either the manifest or the latent goals which the home has set itself.

As is so often the case in human social situations, motives behind behaviour may often be analytically separable, but when it comes to real life can be hopelessly entangled with each other. Thus in spite of those vestiges of the middle-class 'protestant ethic'[2] which seem to imply that medicine is no use unless it is nasty, an activity can be purposive and also enjoyable. In the same way, the daily routines of getting up in the morning and going to bed at night, seeing to one's personal hygiene, taking meals and so on, can be both pleasant and serve some purposes over and beyond those most obviously attributable to them. At the very least, for instance, a daily regimen may minister to a child's sense of security, and inculcate in him habits making for a regular way of life.

Indeed how these routine activities are conducted could be crucial for the general climate of the home. They have a symbolic significance at several levels. For instance there is a strong temptation for busy residential staff to organise them on the basis of operational efficiency: this could save a good deal of time without in any way affecting the service provided to residents. Thus a highly organised showering routine in a children's home could get a large number of children clean and into bed in double-quick time. Yet for deprived children, such as are many of those in residential homes, bath-time can be a time for narcissism: looking at and talking about their bodies; and receiving a little personal attention. To depersonalise it is to make the child feel merely a cog in the machine, and to do nothing at all to restore his already damaged sense of personal worthwhileness. Similarly with getting children into bed. This is a time for quiet and relaxation, and perhaps even for regressing. Even very tough children can be babyish and receptive to the staff as they lie in bed before 'lights out'. It is not a waste of time for staff to be in the bedrooms at this hour, providing children with a sense of being cared for, and an essential part of the social work task for staff who are working within a nurturing regime. Old people also can regress, and enjoy being babied at bedtime.

As already indicated in an earlier chapter, meals can have a very special significance, extending far beyond the nutritional. Psychoanalysts would argue with some justification that they can evoke echoes of infant and mother nursing relationships, and cause feelings about those relationships to be transferred to maternal surrogates in the present.[3] The behaviour of the mother-substitute can thus do something to alleviate insecurities established very early in life. In the light of considerations such as this, greed[4] or a poor appetite[5] gain a new significance. This is not necessarily confined to children. At a more superficial level, meals are important aspects of the general ambience of personal relationships in a home.

Old people often share physical and mental incapacity with the disabled, the chronically sick and other handicapped groups. Getting them dressed, getting them from place to place, getting the washing-up done, and so on, may be achieved more expeditiously by brisk action on the part of the staff, than by encouraging them to do these things for themselves. Not only does self-help take longer, but it often absorbs the time of staff members who have to stand by to give help and advice. And the results are often not very satisfactory. Coats are put on inside out, buttons left unfastened, cutlery may have to be rewashed.

Nevertheless these are inconveniences which ought to be tolerated. Not only may people who cease to practise their social skills soon lose them, but there is also the loss of the sense of independence and of being a person to be reckoned with — of not being merely a pawn, to be moved around the board by somebody else, irrespective of one's own feelings about it. What residential staff have constantly to remember is that what they do about these apparently straight-forward routines often communicates to the client a non-verbal, but what he interprets as a none the less real, comment on him, telling him something of what the worker thinks of him.[6] And the less his confidence, the poorer the view he has of himself, the more likely he is to see the worker's action in a critical and even rejecting light.

The key is probably to try to put oneself in the other person's place. A common failure in this respect occurs in situations like dressing and undressing, taking a bath, going to the lavatory — situations in which individuals living outside of residential homes are able to preserve their personal privacy. Achieving this in the home is not easy, especially where residents cannot manage without some assistance. It is then only too possible to overlook their sensitivity about these matters: to intrude unnecessarily in the interest of convenience, and thus give them just one more indication that as persons they do not really matter. If the result is that they eventually become less sensitive, we have only succeeded in causing them to deteriorate, and thus doing even more damage to them. The attitude of the prison authorities towards the possibility of actually raising prisoners' standards is indicated by the remark of a former head of the British prison service in referring to criticisms of the primitive toilet buckets still in use in cells: 'Prisons were not designed for those from whom this sort of criticism most generally emanates . . . the normal habits of large numbers of the prison population still fall short of refinement.'[7]

The residential worker has only to ask 'How would I feel?' in order to understand how large such matters can loom in the minds of residents.

The use of the word 'routine' then must not be interpreted as meaning 'of no personal significance', and therefore simply to be organised for convenience. These regular vicissitudes of daily life need to be individualised as much as possible, with a proper regard for the feelings of the people involved.

The second kind of activity which must find a place in the daily programme of the residential home is that which provides residents with recreation — in the sense simply of pleasure. What people find pleasurable varies according to age, capability, habits of mind and previous experience. Most of us find it satisfying to use our faculties in our leisure time, though of course some are less well-endowed than others, or have allowed some of their faculties (e.g. muscular or intellectual abilities) to rust through disuse. In other cases there may be culturally rooted habits of mind causing people to reject certain kinds of activity, such as the tendency among working-class residents to recoil from activities like reading serious books or listening to classical music. What many conscientious members of staff fail to recognise is that it is legitimate to reject such leisure-time occupations, no matter how 'good for' residents staff may believe them to be. Skimming through a comic, watching TV or listening to pop music or sentimental ballads are enjoyable to those who engage in them because they touch their feelings and stir their imaginations. Some so-called intellectual activities, alas, appear to leave them entirely unmoved.

This means of course that mainly recreative activities may also fulfil secondary purposes. and thus only imperfectly correspond to Groos's definition of play. They keep the faculties of residents alive by exercise, and often even stimulate them into further growth. One is reminded here of the danger of sensory deprivation in institutions, particularly in institutions for the more immobile residents, to which earlier reference has been made. An active recreational programme may, if incidentally, provide some prophylaxis against this danger. But it may have to be taken directly to the old or the disabled, who will enjoy themselves once they have been stirred from their lethargy. With lively children it may be necessary only to make opportunities available.

A word about what is sometimes called 'escapism'. To some this is a term of abuse. It is, it appears, a moral shortcoming to avert one's face, even now and again, from the realities of life, no matter how grim those realities might be. This is a masochistic creed, and moreover it is an unrealistic one. Few of those who proffer it genuinely practise it themselves. Some of them, for instance, find their own avenue of escape through religion. Even the most determined mountaineers sometimes need to turn aside for a breather in order to continue their journey upwards. Escapism may not be the only purpose to be served in the recreation programme of the residential community, but it is one of them.

The danger in it, is if it becomes a substitute for reality instead of merely a rest from it. Life has to be coped with, and to live in a wish-fulfilling fantasy world all the time can only reduce both one's motivation and one's ability to get to grips with reality. Where this does occur it is not because the programme of a home allows too much scope to the life of the imagination — as we have seen such provision has its own value — but rather the reverse. Sometimes, of course, the problem is personal: residents withdraw into themselves because they have personal difficulties in engaging themselves with reality. Then they need social work (or in the case of schizophrenics, psychiatric) help. But for most, it is an indication that something is wrong with the programme or some other aspect of the regime. When old people in the day room of a home, or old lags in their cells, resort to long periods of apathetic daydreaming, it is a sign that their lives lack interest, stimulation and achievement. So they draw on their own creativity to fill their world with colour and incident and satisfying success. It is a remarkable achievement of the human mind, but an ominously maladaptive tendency nevertheless.

There are finally the 'purposive' elements in a residential programme. Such activities have been introduced not as part of a necessary daily routine, or simply to give inmates pleasure, but in order to realise some objectives of the programme planner.[8] That does not mean that they may not become part of a daily routine. Habit training, for instance, which may well be a social work objective in certain kinds of institution (say for young children, or mentally handicapped persons) would probably necessitate regular and consistent repetition of particular acts if they are to be learned.

Nevertheless purposive, routine training of this kind is distinguishable from the life-sustaining routines referred to above, which are unavoidable in any institution.

Even less, as we have seen, should one define 'purposive' activities as 'not enjoyable'. They may not always be enjoyable. Some protagonists of the 'play way in education' almost imply that learning can always be effortless, and modern education seems only just to be recognising that this is an overstatement of the case. But the more burdensome an activity is, the more essential it becomes to sustain interest in and commitment to it because of the ultimate benefit to be gained from it. For example, physical exercise is burdensome to those who are handicapped, elderly or out of condition. If they are to keep it up, they must feel that there will be some profit from it, which will make it all worthwhile. Vague statements like 'Exercise is good for you' are not usually going to be enough. Specific targets, like reducing your weight, making it easier for you to get about, or alleviating your sciatic pains by strengthening your back, are more appealing and have the further advantage that they represent a clear contract between client and social worker. Having such an understanding between them will oblige the worker to try to realise the (presumably desirable) objective as much as it will motivate the client to persevere with the activity. This kind of accountability may be irksome to social workers, but it is 'of the essence' (as the lawyers would put it) of the social work contract.

In addition there is the motivation to take part in an activity, which is evoked by what behaviour modifiers call 'social reinforcers',[9] such as the expression of approval by the staff or by the resident's peer group. Encouragement or praise by a staff member, or even a smile or a pat on the back, minister to people's need for acceptance, particularly in the case of those (like deprived children) who have lacked such approval in the past; and can provide them with a strong inducement. Peer group pressure can operate either as an incentive to continue or as a deterrent from stopping the activity; and because it stimulates basic anxieties about one's place in the society of the home, it is even more powerful than staff approbation. No one wants to risk rejection by a group with whom one will be spending most of one's daily life. Group discussion and decision methods of the kind described in Chapter 7 would represent ways of establishing group norms in favour of particular activities. They would also establish a kind of contract with residents by ensuring that the case was put to, and critically evaluated by, them as a group. This means of course that the aim of it all would be subject to challenge. In other words, seeking group support is no alternative to clarifying and explaining the object of the activity, but rather an effective way of providing such enlightenment. The use of expressions of approval by the staff, on the other hand, contains no such built-in safeguards. It can be just another form of personal suasion, and is therefore more justifiable as back-up motivation to an approach based on explanation, than as a method for use by itself.

Purposive activities can be divided very broadly into two categories, according to whether the purpose in question is the home's, or the client's. There is a connection between the two of course. Maintaining the stability of a home is a precondition for using it for the client's benefit. Nevertheless they are not the same thing — and sometimes they are not even connected, except possibly negatively. Sometimes peace and quiet in the institution does more for the staff than for the residents. Where this is the case, it is understandable that staff would want to blur the distinction between the two. Often then they deceive themselves as much as (possibly more than) the residents. The need for such self-justification implies guilt, and therefore that something questionable is going on. It would be very much better if a policy which was really aimed at satisfying institutional needs were recognised as such, enabling both its justification and its effectiveness for its real purpose to be properly considered.

It is in this light that a group of activities variously described as immobilising or tension-reducing are to be understood. The tensions which build up in people living in a home may derive from a variety of sources in the regime itself. Thus residents are inevitably limited in the range of personal relationships and of roles which are open to them. They meet the same group of people time after time, which not only tends to intensify those relationships, and therefore to make conflict more likely (and fiercer when it does occur), but also makes it difficult to avoid particular individuals when you want to. The latter can be a source of irritation and stress even if relations with the people concerned are not already fraught.

Similarly with roles. The non-resident has a good deal of scope for varying the way in which he presents himself to others. Thus the man who is bullied by his boss at work can compensate for this by the way he behaves at home or among his friends. In the residential community there is little scope for this 'compartmentalisation of roles'.[10] To a large extent everybody knows you in all your roles, and a degree of uniformity is thus enforced on all your 'presentations of self'.[11] Moreover, the roles available to you may not offer you the activity satisfaction you need. The assembly-line worker outside can seek self-realisation in his leisure activities, but the inmate may be limited to what can be provided within the four walls of the institution.

Of course there is always the possibility of inmates entering into relationships, roles or activities outside the home, and indeed it is only in the most total of total institutions that this will be entirely prevented. Nevertheless it is in the nature of the residential home to be insular to some degree. As we have seen, its justification is in part the protection it can provide to inmates from some of the pressure of the world outside — or sometimes the protection it can give to the world outside from the behaviour of inmates. There will therefore always be a strain towards containment, with its limiting of the range of opportunities available to inmates, to those which can be provided within the home itself.

The lack of enough safety-valves such as these combine with the deprived or unstable personalities of many residents to produce a potentially explosive mixture. Outbursts may occasionally provide dramatic proof that such a problem exists in an institution. Often its effects are more subtle, being discerned in widespread tetchiness among residents, or constant bickering between them. Thus inmates of a maximum security prison (where containment and therefore these tensions are likely to be at their greatest) admit that they overemphasise trivialities, quarrelling over a frying pan, or taking it amiss if a man who has been saying 'good morning' fails to do so one day.[12] When more deeply hidden, such tensions may sometimes emerge only as individual or group resistance to co-operation with other residents or with the staff.

Staff need to be aware of these dangers, and alert to the need for preventive action. The best preventative is obviously to eliminate those features of the regime which are responsible, but enough has already been said to show that they may not always be avoidable. Then it is necessary to consider including tension-reducing activities within the programme.

The value of sports and games as a way of dissipating tension is well recognised. The institution which does not provide adequate outlets for the physical energies of young people is asking for trouble. Because the limitations imposed by the four walls of the institution restrict the amount of physical activity which is possible for residents in the course of their daily lives there, or even required in order to secure the necessities of life, this becomes a very specific activity-deprivation in the residential setting. But quite apart from making up directly for lack of physical outlets by the provision of energy-absorbing recreation, sports and games seem to have a more general value as a way of 'letting-off steam'. Anger, frustration, and a variety of other emotional responses to the residential situation seem to be open to some alleviation by vigorous exercise. The Victorian advice to the sexually frustrated that they should go for long, hard walks provokes only hilarity these days, but it may have some empirical justification.

If this advice ought to be rejected it is probably because it is usually associated with sexual repression, whereas the right way to deal with the problem may be by avoiding unnecessary sexual deprivation. Such deprivation is even less justifiable in the present-day climate of opinion, but it nevertheless seems to be a taken-for-granted feature of life in many residential institutions. Unacknowledged and debatable genetic beliefs (for example that inmates of a home for the subnormal should not breed) sometimes lie behind this. In other cases it is the result of an odd distaste at the idea of intercourse between say old people, or disabled persons. Not to mention a deterrent 'less eligibility' viewpoint which looks askance at the idea of home residents having a sex-life. Enforced celibacy in an institution is often a source of tension and aggression, as well as encouraging people to seek substitute satisfaction through various forms of sexual deviation. Homosexual activity in prisons or one-sex homes is only one example of this.

Physical outlets are obviously not a universal panacea. At both ends of the age range their utility will be limited, as also with the sick or the handicapped. But experience in group discussion therapy has shown that verbalisation is often a useful substitute for action. It has of course a more specific function; you can express verbal hostility towards particular people or experiences in your life or in the institution, instead of, as with sports and games, relying on a kind of generalised safety-valve. To be as specific on the plane of action would involve physical attack directed against the things you did not like — like violence against a hated regime. Hostile expressions of opinion are obviously less disruptive than hostile acts, and (in psychoanalytical terminology) often seem to be adequate sublimations for them.

This is in part a prescription for freer speech throughout the institution. This causes some residential staff to feel very insecure. They seem to fear that violent speech will lead to violent acts whereas the reverse is often the case. To the sensitive social worker the verbal outburst which acts as a stimulus to still greater rage is distinguishable from that which soaks up tension. Indeed, in the former case, the angry person can be seen exploiting the opportunity to denounce his enemies in order to work himself up into a state in which he can risk doing something about it. However, where a relaxed verbal climate is unworkable because it would be too stressful for the staff, or alternatively (as with prisons) where it would conflict too much with the containment role imposed on the institution by public opinion, opportunities can be provided during the daily programme for regular formalised outlets, by means of specific discussion sessions. These might be related to particular aspects of home life, such as menu, recreation, or good neighbour committees, or be discussions held at particular times of the day (say after meals) and used for the ventilation of any matters of concern to residents.

The institutional aim of absorbing tensions can be reconciled with the interests of residents if these discussions are also a means by which grievances can be put right — personal quarrels cleared up and abuses in the home investigated and put right. Many will feel that such procedures then also become more justifiable — more in accordance with the idea of a mutual understanding or contract between client and social worker about the aim of their work together. The role of such problem-solving groups has already been considered in other contexts in this and earlier chapters. As was then shown they represent a sharing of the responsibility for the direction of the home between staff and inmates.

The use of immobilising activities for the control and management of clients may seem to contradict all that has been said about encouraging people to express their conflicts, but this is only an apparent inconsistency. Immobilising activities are those elements of the programme which keep clients in one place — standing at a machine, or seated at a table. As client management techniques they are particularly valuable with hyperactive children, manic patients, or inmates prone to impulsive and irresponsible action (like some mentally handicapped persons) in which they could injure themselves or other people or do a good deal of damage, before any action could be taken to stop them. There are indications from the environment itself which might also make an immobilising activity desirable. Proximity to powered machines or a busy highway are examples. Coping with large numbers of inmates without descent into chaos may also call for some immobilisation, though this will not be the case if grass-roots subdivision into small groups is possible.

But how can immobilising activities (almost a contradiction in terms) not be a denial of the idea of the safety-valve? Unlikely though it may seem the two techniques are at bottom the same. The idea of the safety-valve is that one deflects energy and stress from administratively inconvenient outlets into others which are more consistent with the realisation of the institution's social work aims — or (what alas is not always the same thing) with the peace of mind of the staff. The immobilising activity does this also: transforming hyperactivity, for example, into absorption in a hobby, a parlour game, or a form of work which cannot be carried through without settling down for a while in one place. The function must be absorbing enough to allay the feelings of restlessness which underlie hyperactivity, and therefore probably must contain a substantial element of change and variety if the attention of the resident is not to be lost. In other words, as with the safety-valve, the sublimatory element is essential.

The involvement and needs of the client have inevitably already come into the picture, but it is necessary to remember that impróving unsatisfactory features of the regime or learning to understand other people better or gaining outlets for self-expression through particular elements in the programme, though valuable for him, do not exhaust all his needs. He may have a need for support and encouragement, and sometimes, perhaps, also, to change himself. The literature of group therapy shows that both of these needs may sometimes be satisfied by group discussion,[13] or in the case of the younger or less articulate clients, by activity group therapy[14] of the kind discussed below. Groups can be designed and run to cater for specific client needs in these respects. Thus a residential group who have been helped by the social work staff to develop a mutually supportive norm, will both expect for themselves and try to provide for others a tolerance of shortcomings and failure, and a willingness to help and encourage. Such an attitude may be vital in institutions for the very old and the very young, or for the handicapped where the overriding aim is long-term support and shelter. The group cannot be left to do it all. A setback may even cause the group as a whole to become demoralised, so both for individuals and the group the reassuring words (or sometimes only the reassuring presence) of the social worker is important. Yet as ever, in residential settings, the social worker cannot do it all either. What influence could his occasional morale-boosting interventions have against all-pervading and ever-present deflation by a negatively-minded group?

As a bridge between support and change there is the role of the residential group in strengthening the morale of individuals who lack confidence in their own abilities or in their significance in the eyes of others. An accepting group can encourage them to try again when constant failure has made them reluctant to do so. A tolerant group can allay fears that they will be criticised or even rejected if they do take some positive action. And having succeeded once, such clients will have begun the process of changing the negative self-perception which is at the root of their problems. In the process of supporting other members, such a group can begin to build up a sense of confidence and worthwhileness in themselves. The experience of Alcoholics Anonymous,[15] where the commitment to helping others is so important, is illuminating on this score.

The residential group can be a very potent instrument for further change in all kinds of ways. The coercion from it towards conformity cannot be evaded; the pressure to support your team or to obey the rules of the game is an example of the way this could operate in particular programmed activities. Similarly by bringing such problems to the attention of group members the social worker can ensure that the public opinion of the group is marshalled against malicious gossip, or bullying — to the ultimate benefit of the gossip-monger or the bully. There is also the learning which takes place as a result of interactions with others in the group. This learning is really a gain in insight or understanding as a result of illuminating comments (i.e. interpretations) which people make on your behaviour in the group. Such insight may range all the way from a new understanding of how to do something (which may be as ordinary as how to fill up a supplementary benefits form) to a profound realisation that your lack of success is not the fault of other people, but due to how you yourself behave — and that the latter in turn is the result of vague feelings about yourself engendered in you by an unsatisfying childhood relationship with your parents.

But just as the acting-out of grievances and tensions may sometimes be better replaced by discussion, so conversely may the needs of clients sometimes be better met by a non-verbal activity than by discussion. There is, for example, the widespread need for greater confidence which can be satisfied by achievement in some field of endeavour. There is the need of the hyperactive for the kind of relaxation which comes from some immobilising activity — say one which involves sitting down for a while. The need of some for self-display or fantasy, which can be met by drama activities, or the opportunity to learn to share or co-operate, which participation in a team activity can provide. Competitive games can not only be a solvent for ongoing aggression, but also become a habitual sublimation for it for some individuals. These are the more obvious, but there are more recondite examples in the literature, which are not therefore necessarily less valid. Aichhorn in his famous book, *Wayward Youth*,[16] on institutions for delinquent children, talks about the sublimated satisfaction which a homosexual youth got from working in the tailor's shop.

Artistic activities are often considered to have therapeutic value. The painter can not only express his fantasies and by externalising them, perhaps free himself of them, but also work through his problems by means of his pictures, in which case changes in them will often mirror the changes which are taking place in his attitudes or his emotions. A child in a residential school at first expressed his destructive feelings in a series of gory pictures, but gradually these seemed to become less necessary to him, and the change to more tranquil subjects corresponded with a more peaceable attitude in his relationships with other children and staff.[17] Another child was preoccupied with sex and this was reflected in one inaccurate portrayal of the female anatomy after another. His sexual problems seemed to be alleviated by the opportunity given to him to go on with his drawings (now in a 'dirty drawings book' rather than on the walls), his improvement being marked also by greater accuracy in the pictures.[18]

It should be borne in mind that such activities are not necessarily going to be therapeutic in themselves. Appropriate participation by the social worker will often be required. This may sometimes involve verbal intervention, by encouragement, explanation or interpretation. Sometimes actions speak at least as loud as words: an arm around the shoulders may be even more effective as reassurance. Redl describes this approach as 'action interpretation'.[19] A good example of action interpretation provided in this case by fellow-residents, is to be found in the following incident in Bettelheim's residential school. The children were playing at circuses with their stuffed toys. One of the more aggressive children, projecting his own feelings on to his teddy bear, called it Cinnamon the Dangerous. It had been caught in the jungle and had been eating men and women. The other children took exception to having such a dangerous animal in their zoo, and suggested he changed it into a safer creature; one boy pointed out that all his animals were friendly. The owner of Cinnamon the Dangerous was reassured about the peaceful intentions of the other children towards him, and called his other stuffed animal Calico the Gentle.[20]

There is no certainty that activities of the kinds examined here were solely responsible for any changes which may have occurred in particular clients. Many things will be going on at once in a residential home, and as we have seen they will constitute a recognisable type of regime, i.e. tend to be animated by a common ethos and therefore to have similar effects on residents. This in fact should be the aim: to try to minimise (it will be impossible to eliminate them) those features of an establishment which have effects which are contrary to those aimed at by the regime. Purposive programming for change in clients will form part of a total institutional pattern directed to the same end.

This aim of changing clients is under attack at the moment as an assault on the integrity of the individual. Something has been said in earlier chapters to suggest that subject to the safeguard of the contract it is not only often justifiable, but sometimes unavoidable. The onslaught on the change-role of the social worker usually bypasses those changes brought about in children through nurturing and educating them, possibly because in such cases the necessity is apparent even to the blindest. It is difficult to see any difference in principle. The values taught to children by the social workers and teachers employed in a children's home are the conventional ones for which other social workers are criticised as foisting on their clients. And we all know now that child-training and education are not simply a matter of filling a cognitive vacuum, but involve changing something which is already there, in exactly the same way as does the changing of attitudes in social work.

It is not change as such which should be challenged, but the values which are being instilled in the individuals. And what matters here is not the view about those values of either the social worker or his critics, but of the client himself. The contract ensures his sovereignty in casework. For children the appropriate analogue to the contract is an upbringing in which maximum ventilation is encouraged of the moral issues and the reality situation. The scales are loaded in favour of conventional values in both cases, both because of the intrained and unconscious biases of the workers and the formidable coercions coming from the reality situation in society. The persistence of society requires that this shall be the case. But social workers and teachers should be open-minded enough to convince their clients of the problematic nature of social values: that they do call for justification.

Infant-rearing programmes in a home, developed against a general background of emotional nurture, will have to consist partly of life-sustaining routines: feeding, toilet training, training to avoid dangers and so on. But Freudians have shown us that even these apparently neutral acts have emotional significance, affecting an individual's subsequent personality and attitudes. Premature weaning could lead to the development of an insecure person, grasping at everything, before (as he feels) it is removed from his reach. Toilet training may be easy and produce a relaxed individual, or hard and eventuate in a mean and obsessional character.[21] Social values are also taught more directly, usually in response to infractions of moral or social rules by the child. 'That's not your toy; it's Tom's' is an early lesson on the importance of private property in our kind of society. The child who is scolded for cheating is learning early on to subordinate his individuality to the demands of society — to fit in.

Many children's games teach social lessons, being a kind of self-imposed discipline in which children try themselves out against the demands of life and society. Iona and Peter Opie write:[22]

As long as the action of the game is of a child's own making he is ready, even anxious to sample the perils of which this world has plentiful supply. In the security of a game, he makes acquaintance with insecurity, he is able to rationalise absurdities, reconcile himself to not getting his own way, 'assimilate reality' (Piaget), act heroically without being in danger.

Later education builds on this basis. Where it takes place within the institution, its demands upon the institution's programme will be more formal than those of child-rearing in the pre-school period.

It is not possible even if it were appropriate to engage here in a discussion of the principles of education in the residential community, but three points of particular social work relevance do need to be made. These are concerned with the programme itself and the social context within which it occurs; and the commitment of pupils to it.

There is first of all, the conformist nature of its content: school books reinforce this bias in teachers. Second there is a question as to whether, in a situation in which school and home are so close to each other, the borderline between the two should be drawn as sharply as it is outside. It is sometimes seen as a tragedy that human beings learn so soon to discriminate sharply between work and play, the former being a tiresome burden and the latter pleasurable. Critics argue that this is purely a result of teaching children a stigmatising attitude to work early on, and point to the fact that one man's hated work is another man's cherished leisure-time activity. Leaving aside legitimate individual differences in taste, there is of course the important point that leisure activities are freely chosen and usually make less peremptory demands on you. You can stop when you like, and change them if they pall, in a way which is usually impossible with one's work.

There is, however, a factor which is more specifically relevant to the institutional situation. As pointed out earlier, in this chapter, residential homes provide few avenues of escape from the same round of experiences and relationships. At least a fairly clear demarcation between school and home would provide some possibilities of this kind. The child criticised as lazy or difficult in school would not then carry that reputation with him wherever he went. The child who met one set of opinions about life and society in school, might have a chance of encountering different ones at home. The danger of a reversion to the monistic total institution is always with us in residential homes.

Because it always does have some insular features, the social context for formal education, provided by the home is going to be more impoverished than that of schools outside. The pupils of the latter have a whole society from which they can derive supplementary or compensatory experiences. The more firmly the boundaries of the institution with the outside are maintained, the less the school can take for granted about experiences available to children outside the classroom. The more in other words the school will have to provide them for itself, if it is to fulfil its educational role even as well as schools outside. None of this is intended to exempt the wider environment of the home from its undoubted obligation to provide as rich an out-of-school programme as possible. It is merely a recognition of the extent to which even formal education grows out of and is itself enhanced by the daily experiences of everyday social life.

Some of these problems would loom less large if (as is not always possible or desirable) children went to school outside. What would not be solved, would be the failure of so many schools in and out of homes to capture the interest and commitment of the less able children. Hargreaves[23] and others have documented the alienation from the schools of many lower-stream children, with a focusing of motivations instead on leisure-time activities. This is an aspect of the dichotomisation of work and play to which reference has already been made, but it is less justifiable in a school, which claims to adapt itself to the child mind than in an assembly line or a typing pool. In an institution, alienation from school is even more damaging than it is for children living in their own homes — because the alternatives available to them in their leisure hours are so much more limited. School, it has been argued, may have to compensate for the poverty of out-of-school life. How then can alienation from school be other than seriously depriving?

This chapter has been couched in terms suggesting that organising programmes is the responsibility of the staff. This is in spite of genuflections in the direction of the sharing of some decision-making powers with residents. Such a policy would seem tailor-made for creating passive and dependent inmates. It needs to be supplemented by attempts to stimulate self-directed activity among them.

So staff need to be receptive to suggestions for activities emanating from the inmates themselves. This will mean acknowledging that an activity which appears footling to the staff, may nevertheless be experienced as rewarding by residents. After all there are serious-minded people of impeccable middle-class pedigree in the wider society who devote their leisure hours to collecting and classifying cigarette pictures! Another questionable staff criterion is that the group of residents who are interested in the activity is too small. A group of one is large enough, even if this means that the staff member can make himself available only infrequently — perhaps to get the enthusiast started and help him over his difficulties when requested to do so.

Much also might be achieved in the way of encouraging self-direction by teaching pursuits (like crafts or other hobbies) which residents can if they wish then carry on themselves without needing to attend scheduled sessions at all. In other words, formal activities can be run in such a way as to enrich informal aspects of life in the home. This is an additional gain which may be more important for the fate of residents than anything which individual participants might have got from them.

Chapter ten

Staffing

The quality of the care provided in a residential home depends more than anything else on the calibre of the staff. Yet this aspect often receives very much less attention than the building or the equipment of the home — perhaps because what the staff do is not embodied in a tangible edifice which can be exhibited proudly to visitors or represent a plus in the status contest between local authorities or voluntary organisations. There are examples of a united and strongly committed staff achieving more under adverse material conditions than others, working with less enthusiasm, in shining new purpose-built institutions.

This is not, of course, to make a virtue out of sub-standard accommodation. However, it is the behaviour and attitudes of the staff which makes a reality of the regime of a home, and the regime which determines what kind of life residents will lead, and how they are likely to be affected.

Various kinds of staff role can be identified. There is first of all the role of those concerned with the domestic needs of inmates: looking after their food and clothing, their sleeping arrangements and hygiene needs, and with cleaning the home. At first sight these, though providing an essential background, seem to have little or nothing to do with social work as such. But enough has been said already to show that many of these activities have a symbolic meaning which extends far beyond their more obvious utilitarian significance. Tied up with housekeeping, in other words, is homemaking, and all the associations of belonging and identity, warmth and security which this brings with it.

In our culture (though not necessarily in all) these are feminine and maternal associations. Male and paternal images are more likely to be evoked by the related roles of gardener, and maintenance or odd job man. The use of terms like maternal and paternal should not be taken as implying that such identifications are made only by children. We are talking about the deeper implications of caring and protective roles, which we come to attach to women and men respectively, and the provision of which is as relevant to the needs of mature adults or old people as it is to children.

And, one might add, as relevant to the achievement of the social work objectives of the home as are more specifically social work activities such as groupwork. The question is whether this means that the domestic (including maintenance) staff should be social workers.

The conclusion from research by King, Raynes and Tizard[1] on the residential care of mentally handicapped children would seem to be, 'Yes'. They compare mental deficiency hospitals with children's homes for their success in orienting themselves towards children and their needs instead of towards the 'needs' of the institution; and see the greater success of the children's homes in achieving this as due to the 'household' pattern of organisation which they had adopted. This meant that small units within a home were autonomous, so that (within the limits set by general policy) the head of the unit was responsible for what went on there (like a parent), and that within the unit there was little distinction between the duties performed by different members of staff (like a family). More time was spent on relating to the children than on purely domestic or administrative work, the latter where necessary often being combined with work with children. The more institutional way in which the hospitals operated seemed to be the result of the hierarchical and specialised nature of the medical professions, and be influenced partly also, perhaps, by the detachment, which Isobel Menzies[2] showed to be a functional requirement of nursing as a profession.

The same question may be asked about other staff engaged in work which in itself would not normally be described as social work. There are, for instance, teaching and instructional staff, in a residential school (say for delinquents or handicapped children), or in an institution for adults which has an educational or vocational training element. Heal and Cawson[3] in their research on community homes (correctional, or approved, schools) found that the development of a homelike atmosphere was hampered by the 'school' climate. This tended to be centralised and bureaucratic, in contrast to the household mode of organisation, stressed by Tizard and his collaborators, with its delegation and lack of status distinctions. Heal and Cawson also pointed to the importance attached in writings on teaching, to the maintenance of 'social distance' between teachers and taught. Neither of these features would be conducive to the emergence of a family feeling in the institution. Reference has

121

already been made to the similar problems in connection with nurses.

It is arguable that unlike domestic functions the special requirements of teaching and nursing are such that they cannot be infused with social work values without damage. If this is the case, the only alternative would seem to be the separation of teaching or nursing activities from those of social work, so that both can flourish. This does not necessarily mean that teachers or nurses cannot take part in the social work activities of the home; everything depends on whether they can separate these two roles effectively, both in their own minds and in those of clients. It would be only too easy for the informality of the quasi-familial situation to affect the way clients behave towards staff in the more formal settings of the classroom or of medical treatment, at least for a while, until the consistent maintenance of their two roles over a period had accustomed clients to seeing staff in an appropriately different light at different times.[4] The level of formality would be less in schools or hospitals for younger children, and the contrast with the social work side therefore less marked and easier to accommodate. On the whole, however, it will be the domestic staff whose work will most readily reflect social work attitudes and ideas. In view of the symbolic meaning of many of their duties, it is also important that it should.

Counsels of perfection in child care often outstrip practicability. Thus the role assigned to parents by child care experts would often leave them with very little time or energy for the pursuit of their own interests and the satisfactory realisation of their own lives. Similarly it is impracticable to aim at training all domestic staff in social work. There is no reason to believe that those who are good at doing such things will necessarily find the more intellectual aspects of the training required for social work of interest to them. Nor having regard to the marginality of it in relation to their main, domestic function, would the cost be acceptable to employing bodies?

Much of course depends on the size of the home. In small units staff do follow the 'household' model advocated by King, Raynes and Tizard, but when the unit expands beyond a (Victorian?) family size of, say, ten children to what is for some purposes the perfectly legitimate size of thirty or more, specialisation begins to take place, some being responsible for child care, some for domestic work, etc. To break down such a group artificially into household units would probably restrict the overall level of competence displayed by the staff — nobody is good at everything. And it has the claustrophobic disadvantage referred to elsewhere in the text, of restricting the number of different persons, performing different roles, to whom a resident can have resort as he feels the need.

There is a further doubt about the argument that all should be social workers. Californian research suggests that a social worker's personality may be every bit as important as the social work techniques which he uses, especially if his clients' personalities are such as to match up to his in a mutually satisfying manner. The importance of personality, even in the case of trained social workers, was confirmed also many years ago by research on probation officers carried out by the Home Office Research Unit.[5] Although all the officers, having been trained in a similar manner, saw their work in much the same way, the completion of detailed time-sheets showed that they actually performed in a variety of different ways. As to the importance of matching social worker and client:[6] every residential worker knows that this happens, inmates often gravitating towards those members of staff, whether domestic or social workers, who they feel can best help them at any particular time.

In other words, all may not be lost in a home if domestic staff are not professionally trained for social work. Some spontaneity and some functional staff variability could well be lost (the probation officers, above, notwithstanding) if they are.

Nevertheless one cannot trust the natural instincts of human beings entirely without guidance. There have been plenty of examples of the abuse of residents even by trained staff, especially in institutions for the more defenceless residents like subnormals or old people. Short of this kind of cruelty, carelessness and short-sighted prejudice can also take their toll. It must also be remembered that residents are often so because they need the protection of a residential setting. In the words used by Bernard Shaw in another context,[7] common sense is not enough for them — they need uncommon sense. They make demands on the patience, tolerance and feelings of staff which the untutored staff member may find it difficult to justify, much less to satisfy.[8]

One way of meeting this situation might be to provide non-social work staff with short courses in the elements of social work. These could be relatively undemanding and might be valuable. For domestic staff working in homes for the maladjusted or the mentally handicapped, for instance, to learn what kind of behaviour they had to expect could make their reactions more realistic and effective. It could however remain an inferior kind of preparation for social work, casting its derogatory shadow over the far-from-inferior specialised domestic functions which these members of staff performed. As a short didactically taught course, it would also inevitably be based on general principles, instead of arising out of the practical situations which have to be coped with day by day.

Although not necessarily excluding some briefing of domestic staff on the social work implications of their jobs (training is probably the wrong word) the practical needs of the situation are likely to be better met by treating the social work element as a function which permeates their main role, even though the primary focus of the latter is elsewhere in the life of the home. This function would be realised in their work through the support and guidance given to them by the social workers, who would carry this responsibility in addition to that social work with clients which they carried out directly.[9]

The analogy is with personnel work in industry. In addition to his direct activities in the personnel field, the modern personnel manager is responsible also for the personnel function throughout the undertaking: for seeing, for instance, that the company's man-management policy is carried out by those who are otherwise primarily responsible for supervising production on the shop floor.[10]

Social workers would interpret the behaviour of inmates to domestic staff in a similar way, encouraging them to 'count ten' before launching out in a reaction to such behaviour, supporting them when they found their relationship with clients stressful, and so on. These interventions would also be related to current real situations in the home, and so would eventuate in practical knowledge, knowledge which ran to the tips of the fingers rather than (as is, alas, so often the case with knowledge transmitted through courses) remaining chastely immured in the intellect. This would not necessarily result in an undesirable hardening of status distinctions. The domestic staff are the experts in housekeeping matters, and are usually quite ready to reciprocate from this point of view any advice on social work which they may receive. 'Keep off my clean floor' echoes often and justifiably through many a residential home.

King, Raynes and Tizard point to specialisation on the basis of status distinction as the main impediment to the development of the 'household' mode of organisation. There is no such problem about the kind of specialisation described above. Yet through the personal (as distinct from professional) adjustment to daily social work contingencies, which this approach encourages in individual staff, a variability in the staff behaviour available to inmates is preserved, which more versatile staff roles might have threatened.

There remain for consideration those groups of staff whose main function in the home is social work. A sharp distinction has been drawn in the past between residential social workers, and field-workers, i.e. social workers whose activities are mainly with individuals, families, groups and communities outside of institutions. There are a few exceptions to this. For instance medical social workers do most of their work in hospital, and prison welfare officers are also institution-based. They are not, however, much implicated in the daily life, training and treatment of inmates, but are concerned primarily with the problems which arise as a result of inmates' relationships with people outside the institution — their wives and families, employers, landlords, etc. It is because the daily lives of residents in homes is the focus of the work of residential staff that they have come to be seen more as good parental figures or home-makers than as social workers. This role is contrasted with the casework and other skills attributed to field social workers. The difference in the level of training given to the two groups has tended both to reflect and perpetuate this distinction.

All of this is now beginning to change. On the one hand the more esoteric elaborations of casework skill have lost some of their prestige as the pendulum of social work opinion in recent years has swung somewhat away from the aim of adjusting individuals to fit into society, and in favour of social reform. At the same time, the earlier trend against indiscriminate placement in institutions made it necessary for attention to be given to the proper role of residential care, and the skills required for realising it. A sign of the change in outlook is a recent publication of the Central Council for Education and Training in Social Work, called *Residential Work is a Part of Social Work*,[11] advocating a common training and a single qualification. That the battle is nevertheless not yet won is shown by the ambivalence of the CCETSW itself. Its new lower-level form of qualification, the Certificate in Social Service,[12] seems to have been envisaged as for the generality of residential staff, placing them clearly at a lower level of knowledge and accreditation than the generality of fieldworkers, with their Certificate of Qualification in Social Work. Employing authorities also still have to be convinced. They will second residential staff for professional training in social work, but when they are qualified will often expect them to transfer to fieldwork posts instead of taking their newly-acquired knowledge back into the home with them.

There is a genuine problem here. How sound is it, economically, for the services of an expensively trained professional social worker to be monopolised for some years, by, say, the twelve children in a family-group home, when he could be carrying a case-load in the field which is not only four or five times as large, but in which there is also a constant turnover? In the course of a year, the number of clients for whom a field social worker has provided service might well amount to several hundreds.

In larger institutions fully-trained social work staff would be needed, but though the larger home has its place, especially in short-term care, the fear of the impersonality and mass-methods to which they are prone means that the scope for them is much more limited than it used to be. Small- to medium-sized units, say of thirty, like house units in community homes, also probably require professionally trained staff as unit heads. Otherwise, it looks as though social workers should be appointed as consultants to groups of small homes, charged with the responsibility for the dissemination within them of the social work function in the manner discussed above. If the conclusions of King, Raynes and Tizard about the importance of a degree of unit autonomy for the development of a household atmosphere are sound, they should be consultants and not supervisors in an administrative sense.

What should be avoided is assuming that because such a person is merely a social work consultant and not necessarily himself a residential social worker at this moment, he requires no special knowledge and experience of residential work as such. Social workers, however skilled, cannot be expected to understand the special problems presented for staff in residential care unless they have worked in homes. These special problems arise partly out of the very quasi-family relationships which are seen as the mark of the good home. Substitute parents can be as upset about the problems of their 'families', or as anxious about their own loveworthiness or whether they are doing the right thing as parents in real families. And as in real families, these pressures are usually not confined to a nine-to-five working day, but go on for twenty-four hours a day, seven days a week. They also have to cope as staff of a home with their ambiguous position in the local community, living in it, but only to a limited extent, of it. The articulation of their and their residents' relationships with neighbours and with outside institutions is often a delicate and difficult matter.

In view of the very special stresses to which all staff in residential care are subject, the question of whether they should 'live in' assumes some importance. Seventy per cent of the staff in the forty-four children's homes studied by Juliet Berry[13] were resident. Both points of view are tenable. On the one hand, the 'household model' and the development of a family atmosphere would seem to require that they lived in. The point was made very well by a child who on being told that a staff member was going off duty that moment and so could not help him, replied, 'Well I'm never off duty.' On the other hand, life in a residential community tends to be rather cut-off and artificial. It limits the life and experience of staff, and, as a result, can easily generate unrealistic attitudes within the staff group. Where this happens attachments and aversions are intensified, jealousies often run rife, and parochial matters assume prominence out of all proportion to their real significance. In general, people move around in an ever-narrowing circle, their personalities being both stunted and distorted in the process. This is a form of institutionalisation to which staff who have spent a long time living in institutions are vulnerable, especially those who gravitate into residential work because they have few relationships and interest in outside society, and so seek the family and the life they have lacked within the narrow but protected bounds of the institution.

Where this kind of development occurs it is not only damaging to the staff members concerned, but also to their work with inmates. Because their lives are so impoverished, what they can give to inmates is only a thin pabulum, as well as a point of view which is out of perspective. To protect their own satisfactions, also, they try to erect psychological walls around inmates or other staff which are as high as those which keep them in the institution. Just as addicts seem to need to become missionaries for drug-taking in order not to be isolated in their addiction, so do institutionally dependent staff resent any outside interests among their fellow institution dwellers or the intrusion (as they see it) of the latter's friends and relatives. Everybody must love institutional life as they do.

People like this, of course, should not be recruited to the staffs of institutions, and that in spite of their high level of commitment. Perhaps, even, because of that commitment — because of the fatal affinity for institutional life which it betrays. Also it is important that staff who 'live in' should, like inmates, be encouraged to look outside the home for the satisfaction of as many of their personal and cultural needs as possible.

There is another obstacle in the way of making a reality of the 'household model' in residential care. Families do not change their membership all the time, but the staffs of residential homes often do. David Wills claimed that in one of the homes for which he was responsible he recruited almost as many staff as children.[14] This is not an unusual situation: Juliet Berry, in her research in a number of children's homes, found that one-third had been there less than a year. Such situations result partly from staff leaving, and partly from the practice referred to by King, Raynes and Tizard in which staff are moved around the system of a large institution. Not only does frequent movement from either source mean that experience is lost (or not even gained) but that relationships and growing mutual understanding between staff and clients are constantly frustrated. The worst thing that could happen could be for inmates to be so frequently disappointed by these changes that they give up trying to establish genuine relationships with the staff altogether. As Bowlby[15] and others have shown, this kind of disillusionment in the case of young children can have a serious effect on their subsequent ability to establish relationships of any kind.

A major reason for the high turnover of staff in institutions is undoubtedly the narrow and unrewarding life available to them. Institutions are still too often located in isolated spots. This not only limits the experience available to clients but also the life and satisfactions of the staff. If the society of the institution itself is very introverted and self-contained, the effect can be even more serious. Many people will not stay under these conditions, and many who do are going to be those dependent individuals referred to above who will be most damaged by prolonged residence in an inward-looking institution. If the demands of the 'household' style of home are of this sort, then those demands are probably too great, and we are going to have to be satisfied with rather less.

Research on penal institutions and mental hospitals[16] has indicated how important and how complex the staff group is, as a community within a community. There are often powerful normative constraints within the staff, leading to a monistic staff point of view. In one study of prisons,[17] this staff subculture was found to be even more powerful than the much more widely acknowledged inmate subculture of the prison. This does not preclude disagreements, and almost half of the staff of the children's homes in a recent study[18] were seriously divided on how discipline should be maintained. This kind of disagreement can either lead to no policy at all, or to undercover subversion of the official policy by that section of the staff whose views have been disfranchised. Thus in an open prison studied in the prison research referred to, the dominant staff trend in favour of the inmate participation policy of the governor was countered by a minority opposition view, which was responsible for certain tensions within the prison. Sometimes the split is on a status basis. Incompatibilities may develop between an authoritarian headmaster and his staff,[19] or between basic-grade prison officers and more senior officers, leading to mutual harassment. Where senior staff do not assume responsibility for the consequences of the instructions they give to their subordinates, this buck-passing spreads downwards into the whole staff group of the institution.[20] And if you cannot pass the blame upwards, you pass it downwards on to inmates, who thus become scapegoats for staff, and in particular management, failure.

In these days of paper qualifications for almost everything, the value of staff training for residential social work would seem self-evident. Certainly if there is a body of knowledge to be applied in the field it ought to be taught to those who have to do the work, notwithstanding Juliet Berry's observation that the staff in the better children's units in her research were no better trained than the rest. King, Raynes and Tizard present evidence to show that the *kind* of training is important for determining how the work is done — nurse training leading to a more institutional, and child care training to a more family-centred approach. This is presumably not only because the skills taught in a child care course are more relevant, but also because such a course rejects status hierarchies and the specialisation of functions which appear appropriate to medical treatment but not to residential social work. The training would need to be that of the social worker, and of course embracing the important parts of that training which refer specifically to the residential setting.

But training cannot eliminate the need for careful staff selection. The importance of this has been underlined in one aspect of residential care after another in this and earlier chapters; and is summed up in the view, supported by the research from California, that individual personality is an essential determinant in the way social workers do their jobs and the kinds of clients they can help. This may account for Juliet Berry's negative finding on the value of training. It may not be, as Ms Berry suggests, solely because of the inappropriateness of the training for the job to be done, but because the wrong people are in the wrong places.

So although there are, as we have seen, individuals whose personal needs lead them inadvertently to exploit their work with clients in order to minister to their own needs for acceptance or power, or whose needs are such as to render them vulnerable to the institutionalising process, there are many other, different kinds of individual whose qualities can contribute successfully in one kind of home or another. Thus some who work punctiliously by the book have their niches, just as have those who prefer to take responsibility and exercise discretion in the course of their work. Research on prisons, for instance, suggests that while the former are better suited to maximum security prisons, the latter are better able to adjust to the flux of daily life in an open prison.[21] The qualities of the relationships established within a home have been shown to be of great importance, and the requirements here also can vary a good deal between the intensive individual bond to be established with young children in the nurtural type of institution, and the friendly avuncular relationships of the holiday home. Some staff members can sustain the former, and often this ability arises out of a personal (if controlled) parenting need on the part of the individual involved. Others find this kind of intimacy difficult and embarrassing, but can maintain the more distant kind of relationship with ease. Work with the elderly, the sick, the handicapped or the mentally ill calls for patience and the ability to continue to relate constructively with residents in the face of suffering and death.[22]

Staff training is first of all a means by which an individual can be made aware of the special characteristics which he brings to social work, and the opportunities as well as the hazards which these represent for him, including those which emerge in the residential setting. By itself, this may seem a very limited objective. That clients can develop is one of the expectations which social workers have of them; without such a hope much social work would not be worthwhile. Social workers can hardly expect less of themselves than they do of other people. Self-awareness, then, extends into self-realisation as a social worker, through the development of what are, in the context of social work, one's more constructive social qualities, and the establishment of some control over aspects of one's spontaneous behaviour which are likely to be unhelpful. This is how a well-informed helper is transmogrified into a social worker: by learning about one's self, and then schooling that self to serve the purposes of social work.

So the first emphasis must be on self-awareness and self-actualisation as a social worker. This is the gateway to the realisation of the second aim: the better understanding of clients. In the end, the understanding of other people must be built on empathy: the ability to sense how they feel, and this has to be approached through one's feelings about oneself. Thus to help somebody who is afraid, you must know what it feels like to be afraid.

Two caveats are in order here. The understanding of other people in the light of one's own experience does not mean simply assuming that they feel exactly as you do. Clients will be very different from you: older or younger, more or less mature or intelligent, and having had a very different experience of life. One always does use one's own inner experience to reify one's understanding of others; the cruder projection of one's own feelings on to them is often enough the result, and where not guarded against, becomes one of the commonest sources of misunderstanding between people. Your own self-awareness alerts you to the more urgent needs which might make you want to do this in your social work; and the knowledge of the problems and behaviour of your client group (the elderly, the subnormal, etc.) gained from your training provides an objective framework with which your intuitions have to be reconciled.

The second warning is against a vulgarisation of what has been said above. To argue that you must approach your understanding of others on the basis of your subjective feelings because after all these are the only feelings of which you can have direct knowledge, does not mean that unless you have the same life experiences as them you are impotent to help. You do not have to have a baby yourself (or even necessarily be a woman) in order to be able to empathise with and thus understand a woman who is about to have one. This is just as well, as otherwise the range of cases with which most of us could deal would be severely limited!

The understanding, of yourself and the understanding of your clients, form two legs of the tripod on the basis of which social work must proceed. The third leg is your knowledge of the social resources which can be utilised: the job, housing, educational and recreational opportunities; the human networks available both in the community and the home, to provide clients with relationships, support and stimulation, and the social services which can be marshalled to provide for needs which society would otherwise fail to meet. So training in the social sciences and in the social services is indispensable, but it is the human agent which will make use of this knowledge, and which therefore remains primary.

As long as social work continues to be a process in which one person sets out to help another through the agency of a personal relationship, this is bound to remain the case, no matter how much of the problem may result from unjust laws or an inequitable social system. It may also serve to bring the individual client back into a picture from which he is sometimes in danger of being dislodged by stock figures labelled 'the poor', 'the powerless', 'the workers', and so on.

Notes and further reading

Chapter one: Antecedents

1 Christopher Beedell, *Residential Life with Children*, Routledge & Kegan Paul, 1976.
2 R. Laslett, *Educating Maladjusted Children*, Crosby, Lockwood, Staples, 1977; F. G. Lennhoff, *Exceptional Children*, Allen & Unwin, 1966.
3 R. H. Ward, *The Hidden Boy*, Cassell, 1962.
4 C. Paul Brearley, *Residential Work with the Elderly*, Routledge & Kegan Paul, 1977.
5 *Social Trends*, no. 5, HMSO, 1974, table 25, p. 90.
6 Sir Rupert Cross, *Punishment, Prison and the Public*, Stevens, 1971.
7 Zofia Butrym, *Social Work in Medical Care*, Routledge & Kegan Paul, 1967.
8 W. R. Bion, *Experiences in Groups and other Papers*, Tavistock, 1960.
9 Maxwell Jones *et al.*, *Social Psychiatry: A Study of Therapeutic Communities*, Tavistock, 1952; R. N. Rapoport, *Community as Doctor*, Tavistock, 1967; Stuart Whiteley, *Dealing with Deviants*, Hogarth, 1972, part 1.
10 Maurice Bruce, *The Coming of the Welfare State*, Batsford, 1968, chapter 4.
11 Gordon Rose, *Schools for Young Offenders*, Tavistock, 1967, chapter 1; Howard Jones, *Crime and the Penal System*, University Tutorial Press, 1968, chapter 17.
12 Ivor R. C. Batchelor, *Henderson and Gillespie's Textbook of Psychiatry*, Oxford University Press, 1975, p. 3.
13 John Bowlby, *Maternal Care and Mental Health*, World Health Organisation, 1951; J. Robertson, *Young Children in Hospital*, Tavistock, 1970.
14 Richard Titmuss, *Commitment to Welfare*, Allen & Unwin, 1968.
15 Peter Townsend, *The Last Refuge*, Routledge & Kegan Paul, 1962.
16 C. P. Nuttall *et al.*, *Parole in England and Wales*, HMSO, 1977.
17 K. Pease *et al.*, *Community Service Orders*, HMSO, 1975; K. Pease and

S. M. W. West, 'Community service orders: the way ahead', *Home Office Research Unit Bulletin*, no. 4, 1977, pp. 16 ff.

18 D. Payne, 'Day training centres', *Home Office Research Unit Bulletin*, no. 4, 1977, pp. 5 ff.

19 R. Barton, *Institutional Neurosis*, Barton, 1959; C. Paul Brearley, *Residential Work with the Elderly*, Routledge & Kegan Paul, 1977, pp. 16 ff.; Erving Goffman, 'On the characteristics of total institutions', in *Asylums*, Penguin Books, 1968; Peter Townsend *op. cit.*, chapter 14, etc.

20 J. K. Wing and G. W. Brown, *Institutionalism and Schizophrenia*, Cambridge University Press, 1970, p. 8.

21 Sally Provence and Rose C. Lipton, 'Infants in institutions', in L. J. Stone *et al.* (eds), *The Competent Infant*, Basic Books, 1973, p. 800.

22 J. C. Lilly, 'Mental effects of reduction of ordinary levels of physical stimuli on intact healthy persons', *Psychiatric Research Reports of American Psychiatric Association*, 1956, Vol. 5, pp. 1-9.

23 W. H. Bexton *et al.*, 'Effects of decreased variation in the sensory environment', *Canadian Journal of Psychology*, 1954, vol. 8, pp. 70-6.

24 Provence and Lipton, *op. cit.*, pp. 795 ff.

25 B. L. White, 'Child development research: an edifice without a foundation', in Stone *et al.*, *op. cit.*, pp. 812 ff.

26 Wing and Brown, *op. cit.*, pp. 21-2.

Chapter two: Regimes

1 R. R. Prewer, 'Prison medicine', in L. Blom-Cooper (ed.), *Progress in Penal Reform*, Clarendon Press, 1974, p. 128.

2 R. K. Merton, *Social Theory and Social Structure*, Free Press, 1961, pp. 60 ff.

3 E. Goffman, *Asylums*, Penguin Books, 1968, chapters 1 and 2.

4 G. Sykes, *Society of Captives*, Atheneum, 1968, chapter 3.

5 Howard Jones, *Crime in a Changing Society*, Penguin Books, 1965, pp. 109-10, 115.

6 D. Clemmer, *The Prison Community*, Holt, Rinehart & Winston, 1965.

7 E.g. H. W. Polsky, *Cottage Six*, Russell Sage Foundation, 1962.

8 H. W. Cline, 'The determination of normative patterns in correctional institutions', in N. Christie (ed.), *Aspects of Social Control in Welfare States*, Tavistock, 1968, pp. 173 ff.

9 Howard Jones, 'The approved school: a theoretical model', in J. B. Mays (ed.), *The Social Treatment of Young Offenders*, Longman, 1975, chapter 11.

10 H. W. Dunham and S. K. Weinberg, *The Culture of the State Mental Hospital*, Wayne State University, 1960, chapters 4-7.

11 Isobel Menzies, 'A case study in the functioning of social systems as a defence against anxiety', *Human Relations*, vol. 13, 1960, pp. 95 ff.

12 Howard Jones, 'Dispersal Prison Regimes' (unpublished report to the Home Office, London), 1977.

13 A. T. M. Wilson, E. L. Trist and A. Curle, 'Transitional communities and social reconnection', in G. E. Swanson *et al.* (eds), *Readings in Social Psychology*, Holt, 1952, pp. 561 ff.

14 Personal communication from H. C. Gunzberg, then Educational Psychologist at the Monyhull Hospital, Birmingham.

15 Sir Rupert Cross, *Punishment, Prison and the Public*, Stevens, 1971.

16 *Encyclopaedia Judaica*, Keter, 1972, vol. 10, p. 967.

17 Helen Perlman, *Social Casework: A Problem-Solving Process*, University of Chicago Press, 1957, chapter 6; S. Lorand, *Techniques of Psycho-analytic Therapy*, Allen & Unwin, 1950, chapter 10.

Chapter three: Justifications

1 Clare Winnicott, 'Casework and agency function', in Eileen Younghusband (ed.), *Social Work and Social Values*, Allen & Unwin, 1967, chapter 7; Felix P. Biestek, *The Casework Relationship*, Allen & Unwin, 1961, p. 118.

2 Evelyn H. Davison, *Social Casework*, Baillière, Tindall & Cox, 1965, pp. 14 ff.; Felix P. Biestek, 1961, *op. cit.*, pp. 100 ff.

3 G. M. Sykes and D. Matza, 'Techniques of neutralisation: a theory of delinquency', in M. E. Wolfgang *et al.* (eds), *The Sociology of Crime and Delinquency*, Wiley, 1962, pp. 249 ff.

4 Howard Jones, 'Punishment and social values', in T. Grygier *et al.* (eds), *Criminology in Transition*, Tavistock, 1964, pp. 3 ff.

5 G. B. Vold, *Theoretical Criminology*, Oxford University Press, 1958, pp. 208-9.

6 G. Simmel, *Conflict and the Web of Group Affiliations*, Free Press, 1955, pp. 13 ff.

7 Howard Jones, *The Informed Conscience: In Search of Social Welfare*, Inaugural Lecture, University College, Cardiff, 1971, pp. 13-14.

8 Allen Pincus and Anne Minahan, *Social Work Practice: Model and Method*, F. E. Peacock, 1973, chapter 9.

9 See various references in Gordon Hamilton, *Theory and Practice of Social Casework*, Columbia, 1967. On the general theory: S. Freud, *Outline of Psycho-analysis*, Hogarth, 1959, especially pp. 43 ff.

10 Evelyn H. Davison, *Social Casework*, Baillière, Tindall & Cox, 1965, pp. 38 ff.

11 Calvin S. Hall, *A Primer of Freudian Psychology*, Mentor, 1958, p. 90; Otto Fenichel, *Psycho-analytic Theory of Neurosis*, 1945, pp. 485-6.

Chapter four: Selection

1 R. B. Cattell *et al.*, 'The dimensions of group syntality in small groups', *Human Relations*, vol. 6, 1953, pp. 331 ff. Reprinted in A. P. Hare, E. F. Borgatta and R. F. Bales (eds), *Small Groups: Studies in Social Interaction*, Knopf, 1955, pp. 305 ff.

2 Howard Jones, *Reluctant Rebels*, Tavistock, 1960, pp. 216 ff.; Howard Jones, 'Approved schools and attitude change', *British Journal of Criminology*, vol. 13, 1973, pp. 148 ff.

3 M. Sherif, 'Group influences upon the formation of norms and attitudes', in E. E. Maccoby *et al.*, *Readings in Social Psychology*, Holt, Rinehart & Winston, 1958; S. E. Asch, 'Effects of group pressure upon the modification and distortion of judgments', in *ibid.*, pp. 174 ff.

4   S. Schachter, 'Deviation, rejection and communication', *Journal of Abnormal and Social Psychology*, vol. 46, 1951, pp. 190-207. Summarised in W. J. H. Sprott, *Human Groups*, Penguin Books, 1958, pp. 147-8.
5   Howard Jones, 1960, *op. cit.*, pp. 132 ff.

Chapter five: Order

1   Brian Rodgers, *The Battle Against Poverty*, vol. 1, Routledge & Kegan Paul, 1968, chapter 3.
2   J. C. Flugel, *Man, Morals and Society*, Duckworth, 1945, pp. 169-70.
3   Nevitt Sanford, 'The genesis of authoritarianism', in M. Jahoda *et al.* (eds), *Attitudes*, Penguin Books, 1966, chapter 12, especially pp. 112-114.
4   A. S. Neill, *That Dreadful School*, Herbert Jenkins, 1937, etc.
5   Maxwell Jones *et al.*, *Social Psychiatry: A Study of Therapeutic Communities*, Tavistock, 1952; R. N. Rapoport, *Community as Doctor*, Tavistock, 1967.
6   W. David Wills, *The Hawkspur Experiment*, Allen & Unwin, 1941; *The Barns Experiment*, Allen & Unwin, 1948.
7   F. G. Lennhoff, *Exceptional Children*, Allen & Unwin, 1966.
8   Calvin S. Hall, *A Primer of Freudian Psychology*, Mentor, 1958, pp. 74-8.
9   F. Redl, 'The phenomenon of contagion and shock effect in group therapy', in K. R. Eissler (ed.), *Searchlights on Delinquency*, Imago, 1949.
10 Melanie Klein, *Our Adult World and its Roots in Infancy*, Tavistock, 1962, pp. 11-12.
11 E. T. Bazeley, *Homer Lane and the Little Commonwealth*, Allen & Unwin, 1928.
12 Howard Jones, *Reluctant Rebels*, Tavistock, 1960.
13 *Ibid.*, p. 121.
14 W. David Wills, 1945, *op. cit.*, pp. 50 ff.

Chapter six: Relationships

1   A. H. Stanton and M. S. Schwartz, *The Mental Hospital*, Basic Books, 1954, chapter 15.
2   August Aichhorn, *Wayward Youth*, Imago, 1951, chapter 6; Helen Perlman, *Social Casework: A Problem-Solving Process*, University of Chicago Press, 1957, chapter 6; E. E. Irvine, 'Transference and reality in the casework relationship', in E. Younghusband (ed.), *New Developments in Casework*, Allen & Unwin, 1966, chapter 8.
3   August Aichhorn, 1925, *loc. cit.*; Helen Perlman, 1957, *loc. cit.*; S. Lorand, *Techniques of Psycho-analytic Therapy*, Allen & Unwin, 1950, chapter 10.
4   Howard Jones, *Reluctant Rebels*, Tavistock, 1960, pp. 145-7.
5   John Bowlby, *Maternal Care and Mental Health*, World Health Organisation, 1951.

6   Michael Rutter, *Maternal Deprivation Reassessed*, Penguin Books, 1972.
7   R. Andry, *Delinquency and Parental Pathology*, Methuen, 1960.
8   Calvin S. Hall, *A Primer of Freudian Psychology*, Mentor, 1958.
9   H. R. Schafer, *The Growth of Sociability*, Penguin Books, 1971; K. Danziger, *Socialisation*, Penguin Books, 1971; L. J. Stone *et al.*, *The Competent Infant*, Basic Books, 1973, chapter 6.
10   Howard Jones, *Crime and the Penal System*, University Tutorial Press, 1968, pp. 28-9; Hermann Mannheim, *Comparative Criminology*, Routledge & Kegan Paul, 1965, vol. 1, pp. 304-5; Anna Freud, *Normality and Pathology in Childhood*, International Universities Press, 1966; John Bowlby, *Separation*, Penguin Books, 1975, pp, 411-12.
11   August Aichhorn, 1951, *op. cit.*, pp. 32 ff.
12   Otto Pollak, 'Treatment of character disorders', in Eileen Younghusband (ed.), *Social Work and Social Values*, Allen & Unwin, 1967, chapter 9.
13   Calvin S. Hall, 1958, *op. cit.*, chapter 4; Anna Freud, *The Ego and the Mechanisms of Defence*, Hogarth, 1968.
14   See, for example, W. and J. McCord, *The Psychopath*, Van Nostrand, 1964.
15   Peter Willmott, 'Delinquent subcultures in East London', in W. G. Carson and Paul Wiles (eds), *Crime and Delinquency in Britain*, Martin Robertson, 1971, pp. 98 ff.
16   W. David Wills, *The Hawkspur Experiment*, Allen & Unwin, 1941; *The Barns Experiment*, Allen & Unwin, 1945.

Chapter seven: Change

1   A. F. Young and E. T. Ashton, *British Social Work in the Nineteenth Century*, Routledge & Kegan Paul, 1956, pp. 93-4.
2   Gordon Hamilton, *Theory and Practice of Social Casework*, Columbia, 1967, p. 16.
3   Calvin S. Hall, *A Primer of Freudian Psychology*, Mentor, 1958; Melanie Klein, *Our Adult World and its Roots in Infancy*, Tavistock, 1962.
4   See the various contributions to Howard Jones (ed.), *Towards a New Social Work*, Routledge & Kegan Paul, 1975.
5   H. E. Freeman *et al.*, *Handbook of Medical Sociology*, Prentice-Hall, 1963, pp. 1-165; E. Weiss and O. S. English, *Psychosomatic Medicine*, W. B. Saunders & Co., 1950.
6   For example Edwin M. Lemert, 'Deviance and social control', in L. Radzinowicz and M. E. Wolfgang, *The Criminal in Society*, Basic Books, 1971, pp. 30 ff.
7   Thomas Szasz, *The Myth of Mental Illness*, Harper & Row, 1961, pp. 296-7.
8   H. S. Becker, *Outsiders*, Free Press, 1973.
9   Leslie T. Wilkins, 'The deviance-amplifying system', in W. G. Carson and Paul Wiles (eds), *Crime and Delinquency in Britain*, Martin Robertson, 1971, pp. 219 ff.

10 H. J. Eysenck, *Crime and Personality*, Paladin, 1970.

11 R. Cochrane, 'Crime and personaity: theory and evidence', *Bulletin of the British Psychological Society*, vol. 27, 1974, pp. 19-24.

12 H. J. Eysenck (ed.), *Behaviour Therapy and the Neuroses*, Pergamon, 1960; H. J.   Eysenck (ed.), *Experiments in Behaviour Therapy*, Pergamon, 1964.

13 Winifred H. Hill, *Learning*, Methuen, 1964, pp. 60 ff.

14 *Ibid.*, p. 63.

15 Derek Jehu *et al.*, *Behaviour Modification in Social Work*, 1972, pp. 44 ff.; T. Ayllon and M. Azrin, *The Token Economy*, Appleton, Century, Crofts, 1968; F. Pizzat, *Behaviour Modification in Residential Treatment for Children*, Behavioural Publications, 1974.

16 C. F. Jesness, *The Youth Center Research Project: Differential Treatment of Delinquents in Institutions*, Third Annual Report, State of California Youth Authority, 1970.

17 Eric Berne, *Principles of Group Treatment*, Grove Press, 1966; Eric Berne, *Transactional Analysis in Psychotherapy*, Grove Press, 1961.

18 Irwin Epstein, 'The politics of behaviour therapy: the new cool-out casework', in Howard Jones (ed.), *Towards a New Social Work*, Routledge & Kegan Paul, 1975, chapter 9.

19 B. F. Skinner, *Beyond Freedom and Dignity*, Cape, 1972.

20 C. F. Jesness, 'The Youth Center Research Project: preliminary findings', *Review of Accumulated Research*, State of California Youth Authority, 1974, p. 31.

21 Fritz Redl, 'The psychology of gang formation, and the treatment of juvenile delinquents', in *Psychoanalytic Study of the Child*, vol. 1, Imago, 1945, p. 375.

22 Howard Jones, *Reluctant Rebels*, Tavistock, 1960, pp. 114 ff.

23 R. Lippett and R. K. White, 'The social climate of children's groups', in R. G. Barker *et al.*, *Child Behaviour and Development*, McGraw-Hill, 1943.

24 See the various references in Tom Douglas, *Groupwork Practice*, Tavistock, 1976; also Howard Jones, 1960, *op. cit.*

25 Josephine Klein, *Samples from English Cultures*, Routledge & Kegan Paul, 1965.

Chapter eight: Outsiders

1 Howard Jones and Paul Cornes, *Open Prisons*, Routledge & Kegan Paul, 1977.

2 J. E. Hall Williams, *The English Penal System in Transition*, Butterworth, 1970, pp. 156-8.

3 See the various references in *Day Services: an Action Plan for Training*, Central Council for Education and Training in Social Work, 1975.

4 J. Robertson, *Young Children in Hospital*, Tavistock, 1970; J. and J. Robertson, 'Young children in brief separation: a fresh look', *Psychoanalytic Study of the Child*, vol. 26, 1971, pp. 264-315; J. and J. Robertson, *Film Series: Young Children in Brief Separation*, Concord Films Council, 1967-73.

5 Howard Jones and Paul Cornes, 1977, *op. cit.*, p. 70.
6 Howard Jones, *Reluctant Rebels*, Tavistock, 1960, pp. 154 ff.
7 Juliet Berry, *Daily Experience in Residential Life*, Routledge & Kegan Paul, 1975.
8 Private communication from W. David Wills. See also, M. Bridgeland, *Pioneer Work with Maladjusted Children*, Staples, 1971, pp. 245-6.

Chapter nine: Programmes

1 K. Groos, *The Play of Man*, Heinemann, 1901.
2 M. Weber, *The Protestant Ethic and the Spirit of Capitalism*, Allen & Unwin, 1962.
3 Melanie Klein, *Our Adult World and its Roots in Infancy*, Tavistock, 1962, pp. 11-12.
4 A. P. Noyes and L. C. Cobb, *Modern Clinical Psychiatry*, W. B. Saunders, 1960, pp. 461 ff.
5 Howard Jones, *Reluctant Rebels*, Tavistock, 1960, p. 206; Miriam E. Lowenberg, 'Food means more than nutriture', in R. J. N. Tod (ed.), *Children in Care*, Longman, 1968, chapter 6; an extreme example is anorexia nervosa: Ivor R. C. Batchelor (ed.), *Henderson and Gillespie's Textbook of Psychiatry*, Oxford University Press, 1975, pp. 150-1.
6 F. Redl, 'New ways of ego support in the residential treatment of disturbed children', *Bulletin of the Menninger Clinic*, vol. 13, 1949, p. 64.
7 Sir Lionel W. Fox, *The English Prison and Borstal Systems*, Routledge & Kegan Paul, 1952, p. 229.
8 F. Redl and D. Wineman, *The Aggressive Child*, Free Press, 1968, part 2; R. R. Middleman, *The Non-verbal Method in Work with Groups*, Association Press, 1968.
9 F. Pizzat, *Behaviour Modification in Residential Treatment for Children*, Behavioural Publications, 1974, p. 17.
10 R. K. Merton, *Social Theory and Social Structure*, Free Press, 1961, pp. 371 ff.
11 Erving Goffman, *The Presentation of Self in Everyday Life*, Penguin Books, 1969.
12 Howard Jones *et al.*, *Dispersal Prison Regimes* (unpublished report to the Home Office, London), 1977, p. 338.
13 S. H. Foulkes and E. J. Anthony, *Group Psychotherapy*, Penguin Books, 1957; A. Wolf and E. K. Schwartz, *Psychoanalysis in Groups*, Grune & Stratton, 1962; Howard Jones, *Reluctant Rebels*, 1960, *op. cit.*; H. Walton (ed.), *Small Group Psychotherapy*, Penguin Books, 1971.
14 S. R. Slavson, *Introduction to Group Therapy*, The Commonwealth Fund, 1943; F. Redl and D. Wineman, 1968, *loc. cit.*
15 Alcoholics Anonymous, *Alcoholics Anonymous*, The World's Work, 1957.
16 August Aichhorn, *Wayward Youth*, Imago, 1951.
17 W. David Wills, *The Barns Experiment*, Allen & Unwin, 1948, p. 92.
18 W. David Wills, personal communication.

19 F. Redl, 1949, *loc. cit.*
20 B. Bettelheim and E. Sylvester, 'Therapeutic influence of the group on the individual', *American Journal of Orthopsychiatry*, vol. 17, 1947.
21 Calvin S. Hall, *A Primer of Freudian Psychology*, Mentor, 1958, pp. 107-9.
22 Iona and Peter Opie, *Children's Games in Street and Playground*, Oxford University Press, 1969, pp. 3-4.
23 David Hargreaves, *Social Relations in a Secondary School*, Routledge & Kegan Paul, 1967; David Downes, *The Delinquent Solution*, Routledge & Kegan Paul, 1966.

Chapter ten: Staffing

1 R. D. King, N. V. Raynes and J. Tizard, *Patterns of Residential Care*, Routledge & Kegan Paul, 1971.
2 Isobel Menzies, 'A case study in the functioning of social systems as a defence against anxiety', *Human Relations*, vol. 13, 1960, pp. 95 ff.
3 K. Heal and P. Cawson, 'Organisation and change in children's institutions', in J. Tizard *et al.* (eds), *Varieties of Residential Experience*, Routledge & Kegan Paul, 1975, chapter 4.
4 W. David Wills, *The Barns Experiment*, Allen & Unwin, 1948, p. 68. See also other examples in Howard Jones, *Reluctant Rebels*, Tavistock, 1960, p. 164.
5 Personal communication, Home Office, London.
6 M. S. Folkard *et al.*, *Impact (Intensive Matched Probation and After-care Treatment)*, vol. 1, HMSO, 1974; *Impact*, vol. 2, HMSO, 1976.
7 A contribution by Bernard Shaw, 'Uncommon sense about the war' in the *New Statesman and Nation*, in response to an article entitled 'Common sense about the war', in the same magazine.
8 Barbara Kahan (ed.), *Approved School to Community Home*, HMSO, 1976, p. 42.
9 Barbara Dockar-Drysdale, *Consultation in Child Care*, Longman, 1973, especially chapter 9.
10 G. Strauss and L. R. Sayles, *Personnel: The Human Problems of Management*, Prentice-Hall, 1962, chapter 18.
11 Working Party on Education for Residential Social Work, *Residential Work is a Part of Social Work*, Central Council for Education and Training in Social Work, 1974.
12 *A New Form of Training: the Certificate in Social Service*, Central Council for Education and Training in Social Work, 1975.
13 Juliet Berry, *Daily Experience in Residential Life*, Routledge & Kegan Paul, 1975.
14 W. David Wills, *Throw Away thy Rod*, Gollancz, 1960, p. 69.
15 John Bowlby, *Maternal Care and Mental Health*, World Health Organisation, 1951; John Bowlby, *Separation*, Penguin Books, 1975, chapter 1.
16 Howard Jones and Paul Cornes, *Open Prisons*, Routledge & Kegan Paul, 1977; H. W. Dunham and S. K. Weinberg, *The Culture of the State Mental Hospital*, Wayne State University, 1960, chapter 3.

17 Jones and Cornes, 1977, *op. cit.*
18 Berry, 1975, *op. cit.*
19 Howard Jones, *Group Size in Approved Schools*, unpublished report to the Home Office, 1968.
20 Jones and Cornes, 1977, *op. cit.*
21 *Ibid.*
22 C. Paul Brearley, *Residential Work with the Elderly*, Routledge & Kegan Paul, 1977, p. 45.

Index

Index

Index